WHAT'S THE BIG DEAL ABOUT CHURCH?

WHAT'S THE BIG DEAL ABOUT CHURCH?

Bruce M. Humbert

Critical Mass Books
Haymarket, Virginia

www.criticalmasspublishing.com

ISBN: 978-1-947153-32-5

Cover Design Eowyn Riggins
Interior Layout Rachel Newhouse

CONTENTS

INTRODUCTION
(Please Read)

What's the big deal about Church? This is more than a title for a book. It's a question we all need to consider. After all, the Church is under attack in our day and age more than any time in recent memory. Overall church attendance is in decline, no doubt helped along by the recent pandemic. But things were trending the wrong way long before we started talking about the merits of masks and vaccines. The pandemic became both a magnifying glass and a toxic accelerant to problems that were already confronting the Church. And when I say Church, let me be clear.

I'm talking about the Local New Testament Church.

The list of the things the Church can't do is casually thrown around by critics. As a pastor, I've heard them all down through the years. Things like, the church can't take anyone to heaven—it can't save your soul. That's true, it can't, any more than being in a garage can make you a car.

You don't have to go to a building to worship God. Agreed. But does that mean you should spend Sunday mornings on the golf course? Of course not.

Oh, here's a biggie—the Church is filled with hypocrites. Well, you got me. While I wouldn't say the average Church is *filled* with them, there are people in every congregation who have mixed or ulterior motives for being there. Of course, the same can be said about sporting matches, concerts, and amusement parks—not everyone there really wants to be. Some wives just go to ballgames to make their husbands happy. Some husbands go to the mall to make their wives happy (and to keep an eye how much they spend).

How about this one? The church is always asking for money. Now, the fact is that most churches don't really spend a great deal of time on finances, but I suppose there are examples of some more "mercenary" ministries out there. Churches, however, do need funds to operate.

Have you been to a ballgame lately? They sure ask for a lot of money.

But it doesn't seem to keep the crowd away.

Of course, there is always the good old standby. Church is boring, not relevant, and the services are too long. But did you know that according to the *Wall Street Journal*, in the average NFL game that usually goes on for at least three hours, the amount of time football is actually being played is less than eleven minutes. You read that right. To be exact, it's *10 minutes and 43 seconds*. The rest of the three hours is filled with commercials, replays, coaching, huddling, and styrofoam peanuts.[1]

While there may be a small element of truth in some of the things that fuel cynicism about Church, there are so many other compelling reasons for making church the big to deal to us that it is to God.

First and foremost, *He started the church*. That ought to be enough to make it something important. It was His idea even before the world began. Think about that for a moment. Before kingdoms, civilizations, armies, conquests, and commerce, God had the Church in His mind and plans.

He also *gave His life for the Church*—paying the ultimate price. If you are willing to die for something, it is—by definition—a big deal to you.

In addition, *God meets with His church*, even if it is just two or three people. *He also empowers His church*, and *receives glory from her*. The Church is referred to as His bride and *He loves her*.

There's no way around it—the Church is a very big deal to God!

I have written this book because of all-too-common errors about the Church, even among professing Christians. Most of these have come about because His bride has been misrepresented, often by so-called spiritual leaders who should know better. My goal is to remind all people who love God, and have a desire to know Him better, that understanding how big of a deal the Church is to Him is crucial to their spiritual life and growth.

In this book, I deal with eight fundamental characteristics about His Church. I believe a grounding in these things will help God's people grasp vital doctrine and defend Christ's beloved bride to both misinformed Christians and the watching world.

Pastor Bruce M. Humbert

Richton Park, Illinois

July 2022

---

[1] "11 Minutes of Action," David Biderman, *Wall Street Journal*, January 15, 2010

CHAPTER ONE

"The PARADOX of the Church"

Most of us love a good mystery—Agatha Christie, Alfred Hitchcock, Sherlock Holmes. There's something about trying to figure out who did it. It's addictive. Of course, not all mysteries are fictional. History is filled with unsolved puzzles. I find it refreshing when something that is clearly defined as a mystery is unraveled, and the solution is clear.

The Bible talks about several mysteries. There is the mystery of our future glorified state ("Behold I show you a mystery," I Corinthians 15:51) and the mystery of Christ living in us (Colossians 1:27). The great thing about Biblical mysteries is that God ultimately gives us the solution.

One of the greatest mysteries in scripture is something prophets in the Old Testament talked about and Jesus spoke about in his earthly ministry. But ultimately, it was the Apostle Paul who was charged with solving the mystery for us, once and for all:

> *"How that by revelation he made known unto me the mystery; (as I wrote afore in few words, Whereby, when ye read, ye may understand my knowledge in the mystery of Christ). Which in other ages was not made known unto the sons of men, as it is now revealed unto his holy apostles and prophets by the Spirit; that the Gentiles should be fellow heirs, and of the same body, and partakers of his promise in Christ by the gospel:"*
>
> —Ephesians 3:3-6

He was, of course, talking about the mystery of the CHURCH—clearly a big deal.

A little later in the same epistle, Paul wrote:

> *"Wives, submit yourselves unto your own husbands, as unto the Lord. For the husband is the head of the wife, even as Christ is the head of the church: and he is the saviour of the body. Therefore as the church is subject unto Christ, so let the wives be to their own husbands in everything. Husbands, love your wives, even as Christ also loved the church, and gave himself for it; That he*

might sanctify and cleanse it with the washing of water by the word, That he might present it to himself a glorious church, not having spot, or wrinkle, or any such thing; but that it should be holy and without blemish. So ought men to love their wives as their own bodies. He that loveth his wife loveth himself. For no man ever yet hated his own flesh; but nourisheth and cherisheth it, even as the Lord the church: For we are members of his body, of his flesh, and of his bones. For this cause shall a man leave his father and mother, and shall be joined unto his wife, and the two shall be one flesh. This is a great mystery: but I speak concerning Christ and the church. Nevertheless let every one of you in particular so love his wife even as himself; and the wife see that she reverence her husband."

—Ephesians 5:22-33

Abraham had been called by God to be the Father of a great nation, one that would declare the true God to a fallen and depraved world. Two thousand years later, Christ came into the world, and at the point of His finished work—death, burial, and resurrection—that great nation was temporarily set aside in favor of something brand new—a new body of people, not limited to one race, or nation, or culture. This new body was designed to proclaim God's glory and the Gospel of Jesus Christ.

An Intimate Illustration

In the Ephesians chapter five passage, God uses the relationship of a husband and wife to illustrate vital things about the intimate relationship between Christ and His church. He uses marriage to reveal the mystery of the relationship between the church and Jesus Christ. He is the head of the church. He is the savior of the church. He gave His life for the church. And He wants to cleanse and work in the church to make her glorious.

That's what makes the church a big deal.

The New Testament declares the mystery of the church, yet the enemy has done his devilish best to keep the truth hidden and misunderstood in each generation. How many of you have friends or family you have invited to church, only to be told the church is full of hypocrites and that they can worship God at the lake as much as in a building? It's clear that too many today don't have a high opinion of something so near and dear to our Lord's heart.

Timing to a book is what location is for real estate. And now is the right time for a fresh look at the local

New Testament Church. Of course, one reason for this urgency is the COVID-19 pandemic, which has rocked every aspect of our lives— our jobs, schools, homes, and churches.

As we slowly emerge from the crisis, and with all the risks for setbacks, the state of the church in American life is nothing short of perilous. Of churches meeting in person, about one-third of pastors report attendances of roughly 50% compared to a year earlier. And Sunday School classes and small groups have been even slower to come back, as well. Smaller churches have struggled the most.1

In other words, churches across America are hurting.

Flawed Thinking about the Church

People have all sorts of misconceptions about the church. Some of these are simply due to a lack of Biblical understanding. But some of them come from so-called teachers who, for their own reasons, minimize the importance of churches, usually in favor of their own preferred substitute. And now, with so many people growing accustomed to virtual church, never in modern times has it been more important to issue a clarion call about the New Testament Church.

Among the errors are some that have been around for centuries. For example, the idea promoted by our Roman Catholic friends who claim Simon Peter founded the church. No, he didn't! As the great anthem says, "The church's one foundation is Jesus Christ our Lord."

People ask, *"What's the big deal about the church?"* They say, "We all believe in the same God, and we're all going to be with Him someday, so why all the fuss about all these different churches?" This illustrates the masterful job the devil has done manipulating the issue and deceiving so many. What God has designed as a mystery that has been revealed, the enemy desires to keep shrouded in a cloud of controversy and confusion.

I'm a Baptist

As a pastor, I feel the need to be very basic in my teaching, preaching, and writing about the church. I do this on purpose because I want people to see with their own eyes and understand this great truth with their own minds. I also want you to know that I am an unashamed and unapologetic Baptist. My ministry has been spent as a Baptist pastor and evangelist.

But I have ministered to many Baptist church members who are not really Baptist in their hearts. They have never really studied the scriptures on the subject, and they don't really know why they identify as Baptist. I want to help with this. I am particularly concerned about young people. I see so many falling away as they grow up and leave home. While others stay in the faith but move on to congregations that don't stand for the same things that were taught in their Baptist heritage.

Now, I know some simply want to be around more people in their age group as the people of some Baptist churches grow older. I get that. But there is something vital to be said about the church being "inter-generational." There are many things younger people can learn from older people, and also there are many things older people can learn from younger people. If we can ever find ways to blend the maturity and wisdom of the elders in the church with the vision and passion of the younger people, well, the world should watch out.

Let me begin by clearing up the paradox of the church. Here's what Jesus said about it:

> *"When Jesus came into the coasts of Caesarea Philippi, he asked his disciples, saying, 'Whom do men say that I the Son of man am?' And they said, 'Some say that thou*

> *art John the Baptist: some, Elias; and others, Jeremias, or one of the prophets.' He saith unto them, 'But whom say ye that I am?' And Simon Peter answered and said, 'Thou art the Christ, the Son of the living God.' And Jesus answered and said unto him, 'Blessed art thou, Simon Barjona: for flesh and blood hath not revealed it unto thee, but my Father which is in heaven. And I say also unto thee, That thou art Peter, and upon this rock I will build my church; and the gates of hell shall not prevail against it. And I will give unto thee the keys of the kingdom of heaven: and whatsoever thou shalt bind on earth shall be bound in heaven: and whatsoever thou shalt loose on earth shall be loosed in heaven.'"*
>
> —Matthew 16:13-19

The Lord Jesus said to Peter that His church would be built on a rock, that being Peter's powerful spirit-driven confession—"Thou are the Christ." Jesus was the anointed one, the Messiah.

The Church is an ASSEMBLY

The word church is translated from Greek (the language of the New Testament), and the word is *ekklesia*, which means "a called-out assembly." It was actually a prevalent word when Jesus walked the earth. It could refer to a crowd—or even a mob. It could refer to people gathered at Soldier's Field to watch the *Chicago Bears*. It's a generic term. But God has this way of co-opting the ordinary and filling it with meaning and significance.

Jesus used it for a different kind of "assembly," one filled with people answering the call of God. The word is used 114 times in the New Testament. And every single time, it means assembly. It is used in three ways: an institutional sense, a local sense, and a glorified sense.

When Jesus, in Matthew chapter 16, said that He was going to build His church, He was speaking of it in an institutional sense. For example, when I make a statement like, "the American family is suffering today," I'm not suggesting that there is one American father and one American mother and all the rest of us are their little darlings. Of course not. I'm speaking of "family" in a purely institutional sense, where the term "family" represents many actual families.

The word church is also used in a glorified sense. This involves the future. One day the great trumpet will sound, and the assembly that has been called out of the world, in the sense of being a people sanctified and separated as a vessel to be used by the Lord to proclaim

His gospel, will be gathered in heaven as described in the Book of Hebrews:

> *"But ye are come unto mount Sion, and unto the city of the living God, the heavenly Jerusalem, and to an innumerable company of angels, To the general assembly and church of the firstborn, which are written in heaven, and to God the Judge of all, and to the spirits of just men made perfect,"*
>
> — Hebrews 12:22-23

The Church is a LOCAL Assembly

The main takeaway from all of this is that the word, church, in the New Testament is used primarily and overwhelmingly in a local sense. The local New Testament church. It refers to a literal assembly gathered in specific places. There was the church at Ephesus, another at Corinth, and so forth. I came from a great church in Akron, Ohio. It was a specific, literal, and visible local assembly.

The word itself doesn't tolerate any idea of a "universal" or "invisible" church. It must be local because individual people can't be assembled in more than one locale. The word clearly implies something being assembled. For example, an automobile is made up of many parts, but they have to be put together. How good would a car be if you had a fender in one place and a number in another place? Assembly means just that—something assembled. In the New Testament, the word is used 99 times in connection to a specific geographic location.

When you get to the eighteenth chapter of Matthew, Jesus talks more about the church and how it can be part of problem-solving:

> *"Moreover if thy brother shall trespass against thee, go and tell him his fault between thee and him alone: if he shall hear thee, thou hast gained thy brother. But if he will not hear thee, then take with thee one or two more, that in the mouth of two or three witnesses every word may be established. And if he shall neglect to hear them, tell it unto the church: but if he neglect to hear the church, let him be unto thee as an heathen man and a publican."*
>
> — Matthew 18:15-17

"Tell it to the church," He said. This clearly implies a tangible, visible, specific entity. If the church is "everywhere," how will you take anything to it? Where would you go?

> *"And great fear came upon all the church, and upon as many as heard these things."* — Acts 5:11

"I commend unto you Phoebe our sister, which is a servant of the church which is at Cenchrea." — Romans 16:1

"For first of all, when ye come together in the church, I hear that there be divisions among you; and I partly believe it." — I Corinthians 11:18

"(For if a man know not how to rule his own house, how shall he take care of the church of God?)" — I Timothy 3:5

These verses clearly describe literal assemblies with real people gathering in real places. In Acts chapter seven, Stephen talked about the "church in the wilderness" before the Sanhedrin. He was speaking about the ancient nation of Israel—real people in a real place. Even the metaphors in the New Testament speak of a tangible church. How can a body be a body if its parts are dismembered? How can it be a building or a bride?

The Church is a Visible, Local Assembly

Many theology textbooks make a big deal about how the church is "universal." They see this as the main thing, with actual local churches being more of a footnote. But that is not what the scriptures really teach. There are voices on the radio and in podcasts and faces on television and computer screens that seem determined to devalue the local church. But they have their own agendas.

Even some evangelicals today are hurting more than helping the church. The promotion of the church as a phantasm—something not visible or tangible—does a great disservice to Biblical truth. The false notion of a "universal" church dates back centuries and has its roots in Roman Catholicism. The very word "catholic" means "universal." They meant back then that it was visible but with many locations throughout the world.

Then the reformer Martin Luther came along. He hated the Catholic Church (and the feeling was mutual) so much that he was determined to promote the opposite of whatever they said. So, if Roman Catholicism said the church was universal and visible, Luther said it was universal and invisible. And this very bad idea is entrenched in evangelical teaching today.

How often have you heard someone say, "We make up the church"? They are confusing the "family of God" with the church. The concepts are not synonymous. The true church is both local and visible. Period. We are commanded as a church to solve problems. We are commanded to serve. We are commanded to take care of the church. How can we do this if there is no specific and tangible church?

The New Testament church is given pastoral leadership to ensure good behavior. It is not random or hodgepodge. It is not a mob of confusion. There is structure and organization. There are specific components. It must be constituted.

In Acts chapter two, we see a definition of the constituency of the church:

> *"Then they that gladly received his word were baptized: and the same day there were added unto them about three thousand souls."*
>
> —Acts 2:41

So, to be part of, a member of the church, first of all, you must be saved. You must have "gladly received" the word. When people talk to me about joining the church, my first question is about their salvation experience. To be a member of an authentic local New Testament church requires this.

The next clear Biblical requirement is baptism. Some people suggest that making a big deal about this keeps many away from the church. But I'm not the one making a big deal of it—God is. God's order is clear: belief, baptism, and belonging.

I find it strange that a true believer will resist water baptism. The late Harry Ironside, who for many years pastored the famous *Moody Church* in Chicago, used to say that an unbaptized believer was a contradiction in terms. He was right.

Baptism in water is the first act of obedience for a true believer and follower of Jesus Christ. So, it is no wonder that this, too, is undermined and often under attack. Some say you can be baptized as a baby, and that puts you in the family of God. Others say water baptism is how you get saved.

So many evangelicals in the Christian media world promote the whole universal, invisible church idea. They use the term church to describe the entire family of God. There are many positive things to be said about Christian radio. It sure beats about 99% of the rest of the media junk out there.

When it comes to this false idea of the so-called universal church, there are many damaging side-effects. First, it undermines faithfulness to one's local church. Second, it promotes church "hopping." Third, it strengthens parachurch organizations at the expense of the church. Such organizations may proclaim they're there to help the church, but sometimes they become parasites—just feeding off it.

There are, of course, parachurch ministries that do, in fact, help the church. AWANA is a great example. It's a great tool for churches. But no parachurch ministry should ever dictate, control, or replace the local church.

Many of my pastor friends started Christian Schools in their churches. But because of poor organization and people loving the school more than the church, the tail has wagged the dog. It drains the time, energy, and financial resources away from the local church.

False teaching about the church leads to compromise. When this happens, the very distinctives that make a local church strong and pure are put at risk. This leads easily to ecumenicism, which waters down so many essential Biblical doctrines.

Another damaging impact of the teaching of a universal church is that it tends to erode genuine church discipline. People can bounce from church to church without resolving their conflicts or cleaning up their lives.

When the scriptures aren't clearly taught, new believers are distracted from the first vital act of obedience—water baptism. The whole "invisible/universal" church myth is also related to another fiction—the substitution of Holy Spirit baptism for water baptism.

I realize that some people don't like being tied to one church, but this demonstrates flawed and unbiblical thinking. Maybe they've never been taught, or what they were taught was wrong. Membership in a local church means you've made an important commitment. It means you need to show up. It means you serve. It means you contribute.

Too many Christians are supporting parachurch organizations at the expense of the local church. My Dad used to say to me, "Just think of the millions of dollars that have been sent" to a particular Christian organization. These organizations are always asking for money. I remember he would say that when so and so passed on (leader of this particular organization), the epitaph on his tombstone would be Luke 16:22: *"And it came to pass, that the beggar died..."*.

The Church is HIS Visible, Local Assembly

Jesus said He would build HIS church. How could anything be more clear? The local church doesn't belong to a denomination. Some denominational board of directors can't dictate policy or convictions to the local church. We see this happening all the time. Issues like the ordination of women and accepting same-sex marriage are being dictated by some central denominational authority, regardless of what a local congregation in the denomination might want or irrespective of what Jesus Christ clearly wants as revealed in His Word.

When the Bible says that the bishop must be the husband of one wife, it makes it pretty clear that the bishop is to be a man. No denominational board has the right to dictate that a local church must have a woman pastor or be gay-friendly. They simply don't have that kind of authority—at least not in the eyes of our Savior.

The church also doesn't belong to a Pope or even a pastor. It doesn't belong to a priest. The church doesn't belong to a rabbi. In fact, the church doesn't belong to anything in and of this present world.

The church belongs to Christ. Period.

Twelve Earmarks of an Authentic Local Church

1. The local church's founder and the head is Jesus Christ. It's not Buddha, nor the angel Moroni, as with the

Mormons. And it's not Mohammed (Matthew 16:18, Colossians 1:18).

2. The local church's only rule, the final authority in faith and practice, is the Bible (II Timothy 3:15-17).

3. The local church's name is "church," and it is called "Baptist" by baptism. If they baptize you as an infant in the Roman Catholic church, you're a Catholic. We are Baptist because of our baptism—it's not a name that will get you into heaven. It simply distinguishes our doctrine (Matthew 16:18, Revelation 22:16).

4. The local church's polity is congregational. This means that all members are equal. When you think about it, the early church practiced democracy long before anyone in Western Civilization (Matthew 20:24-28 & 23:5-12).

5. The members of the local church are truly saved and scripturally baptized (Ephesians 2:21, I Peter 2:5, Matthew 28:19, & Acts 2:41).

6. The local church's two ordinances are baptism and the Lord's Supper. These have no power to save, and they are not sacraments. There are only two—not seven, and they contribute nothing to our eternal destiny—they are simply powerful symbols of Biblical truth (Matthew 28:19-20 & I Corinthians 11:23-34).

7. The local church's officers are pastors and deacons. The words pastor, bishop, and elder are interchangeable (I Timothy 3:1-16 & Acts 20: 28). In the Acts passage, the words "flock" (led by shepherd or pastor) and "overseers" (from the Greek word for bishop) are both used as Paul addresses the "elders."

8. The local church's work is evangelism—winning souls, baptizing those converts, and teaching members, which is true Biblical discipleship (Matthew 28:16-20).

9. The local church is supported financially by tithes and offerings from its members (I Corinthians chapter 8-10).

10. The local church's weapons are spiritual, not fleshly (II Corinthians 10:4 & Ephesians 6:10-20).

11. The local church is independent from the control of the government, the world, religious authorities, and any other organizations ((Matthew 22:21).

12. The local church's preservation is forever (Matthew 16:18).

Three-Fold Criteria for an Authentic Church

The first criteria is the Bible—God's Holy Word. It speaks clearly of a congregation made up of saved people,

people who know Jesus, the founder of the church. If He didn't found the church, it's not authentic.

This rules out:

* *Roman Catholicism, founded around 250 A.D., by Pope Leo.*
* *Easter Orthodox, founded in 869 A.D.*
* *Protestant Churches (out of Roman Catholic via the Reformation, c. 1550s)*
* *Lutheran (1517—Luther)*
* *Anglican/Episcopal (1534—Henry VIII)*
* *Reformed (1534—Calvin, Switzerland)*
* *Presbyterian (1560—Knox, Scotland)*
* *Congregational (1580)*
* *Moravian (1727—Zinzendorf, Moravia)*
* *Methodist (1739—Wesley, England)*
* *Brethren (1830—J.N. Darby, my dad went to a Brethren church as a boy)*
* *Church of Christ/Christian (1830—Alexander Campbell, USA)*
* *Foursquare (1918—Aimee Semple McPherson, USA)*
* *Bible Church (1930—McCarrell, USA)*

The second criterion is the baptism—the entrance to a church. When Paul wrote to the Corinthian church about being baptized by one Spirit into one body (I Corinthians 12:13), he was reminding them that they had been baptized into the church at Corinth. It was baptism authorized by the Spirit of God. This ensures that the church is made up of a regenerate membership.

The third criterion for an authentic church is the behavior. The Bible clearly teaches that we are to submit to those who have the rule over us because *"they watch for your souls"* (see: Hebrews 13: 7 & 17). The church doesn't exist just so we can have an emotional lift every weekend.

The church exists to glorify God.

> *"Now unto him that is able to do exceeding abundantly above all that we ask or think, according to the power that worketh in us, Unto him be glory in the church by Christ Jesus throughout all ages, world without end. Amen."*
>
> —Ephesians 3:20-21

This means the church is the best place you can be. And if indeed God has brought you, you should certainly stick around. You should stay. You should not but be steadfast about your local church commitment. And if you ever do decide to move from a local church, it should be only for the most serious of reasons, for example, if a church departs from solid doctrine. You should never leave over issues of personality or mere preference, certainly never over matters of pride and ego.

In fact, the local church is so important, I think you should make what church you will commit to the most significant part of your decision when relocating to another city or state. Never become a church hopper or sermon sampler. That falls far short of the glory of God.

Members of His church should make every effort to be faithful in all things. I remember having a conversation one time with a family. They told me that they loved our church. I asked them why then were they not faithful in attendance. They got defensive and said they do their best to come on Sunday mornings, but they have other commitments that keep them from going much beyond that. They didn't get involved in ministry, and they didn't serve at all.

I asked them how it would be if I said I loved my family, but I only show up at home once a week? That would get old very soon. I could protest my love, but it would ring hollow because my actions showed weak commitment.

It's His church. This fact, by definition, makes the church a big deal. When God adds me to His church, I'm staying, serving, and striving to glorify Him in that church!

---

1 The State of Church Attendance as Covid Turns One, Trevin Wax, The Gospel Coalition Blog, February 23, 2021

CHAPTER TWO

"The PRIORITY of the Church"

The *Barna Group* conducted a survey examining the changes in church attendance habits due to the COVID-19 pandemic.[1] The research showed that one in three practicing Christians has stopped attending services. The survey also indicated that 35% are still attending their pre-COVID church, 32% are no longer attending, and 14% percent have switched to a new church. Also, it will come as no surprise that 18% are watching online services from different churches each month. In addition:

* 50% of Millennials have stopped attending church.
* 17% of Generation X attend a new church.
* 40% of Baby Boomers stayed at the same church.

In other words, more and more Americans seem to have a cynical answer to the question: *"What's the Big Deal about Church?"* A few years back, another survey by the same company indicated that only 25% of adults who have a Biblical worldview believed the church was central to someone's spiritual growth.

We need to rediscover the *PRIMACY* of the church. In other words, the local church must be at the top of any list of priorities for believers. This means it must be more than prominent—it must rank first.

Over the years, I've been blessed by so many faithful church members under my ministry. I am quite certain it's not because I'm so wonderful or charismatic. I hope people have been faithful because they wanted to bring honor and glory to Jesus Christ. But it's glaringly apparent that, when it comes to the total number of people who profess faith in Christ, my church members were in the minority. Frankly, it's incredible how people think contrary to what God's Word clearly teaches, which is the primary reason I have written this book.

Maybe some of us preachers are at fault because of training that has not effectively prepared us to see the value of the local church as a doctrine. Possibly, they've just become weary of trying to persuade immature—and in some cases, actually unsaved—members. But before we criticize them too much, we should think like parents. I mean, how many moms and dads have worked with a troubled child to the extent that they want to throw their hands up and declare, "I quit!"

Preachers feel that way sometimes.

The Apostle Paul warned young Pastor Timothy about this very thing:

> *"For the time will come when they will not endure sound doctrine; but after their own lusts shall they heap to themselves teachers, having itching ears; And they shall turn away their ears from the truth, and shall be turned unto fables."*
>
> — II Timothy 4:3-4

This generation likes to talk—and talk. People love the sound of their own voices and are passionately in love with their opinions and "feelings." It makes them feel good.

A few years ago, when Oprah Winfrey still had a daily television show, I happened to be in a car wash waiting room while my vehicle was being given a thorough scrubbing and her program was on television. Now, I know she is like a goddess to many people, even an idol. But she is the poster-child for the point I want to make.

She was interviewing a mother who had given birth to a daughter, but by the time the girl was seven years old, the daughter "realized" that she was not actually a girl but rather a boy trapped in a girl's body. Now, the girl-boy was sixteen years old, and the mother allowed her to have a mastectomy so she could be physically changed to being a boy. Oprah applauded their courage and commended them, adding a comment about how hard it was for her to believe that there were still people who couldn't accept the fact that people are born gay and that God created them that way. Of course, nothing could be further from the truth, but that's what happens when preachers don't have the guts to stand up and capture the attention of their eternity-bound audiences.

Preaching is serious business. But the average preacher falls far short when it comes to proclaiming the truth about sin. So, it should come as no surprise that these same failed preachers don't see the value of teaching about the doctrine of the church. These days, preachers not only need to know their Bibles, but they also need intestinal fortitude—good old-fashioned guts.

Like one preacher I heard about—he was so determined to get the truth out to his people about the dangers of alcohol and tobacco that he came up with a compelling visual demonstration idea. He had three jars on a table on the platform. The first was filled with alcohol, and he put a worm in it. The second jar was filled with another worm, along with cigarette smoke, and had a lid. The third jar was filled with another worm, along with soil. He went on to preach about what drinking and smoking did to the human body and then pointed to the dead worm in jar one and another dead worm in jar two. Of course, the worm in the third jar was thriving.

The preacher wanted to know if his congregation was getting his point, so he asked them: "What can we learn from this demonstration?" Without any hesitation, a little old lady sitting in the back put her hand up and said, "As long as you drink and smoke, you won't have worms."

That preacher would have been better off sticking to preaching and leaving the science experiment alone.

The fact of the matter is, no matter how hard I preach, how much of my heart I pour into a sermon, if the hearer ignores the Holy Spirit, He is grieved and quenched. In such cases, people can leave church worse than when they came in. So, it's vital to give an ear to what God is saying.

> *"For this cause I bow my knees unto the Father of our Lord Jesus Christ,*
>
> *Of whom the whole family in heaven and earth is named, That he would grant you, according to the riches of his glory, to be strengthened with might by his Spirit in the inner man; That Christ may dwell in your hearts by faith; that ye, being rooted and grounded in love, May be able to comprehend with all saints what is the breadth, and length, and depth, and height; And to know the love of Christ, which passeth knowledge, that ye might be filled with all the fulness of God. Now unto him that is able to do exceeding abundantly above all that we ask or think, according to the power that worketh in us, Unto him be glory in the church by Christ Jesus throughout all ages, world without end. Amen."*
>
> — Ephesians 3:14-21

The church is very special to the heart of God. It's called the Bride of Christ. It's called His Body. Jesus started it and gave himself for it. And He's preparing a place for her in heaven. To our Lord, the church is, in fact, a very big deal. If a man says he loves God but dismisses or devalues the church, he deceives himself. Or maybe he is just ignorant.

If you say you love me, but you can't stand my wife, we will not be close friends. It's the same with the church. It's Christ's bride, and to say that you love Jesus, but not His church is, well, not the brightest thing to say or do.

There is a danger of losing sight of the church in the process of emphasizing the building of the kingdom of God. We desire to reach lost people and introduce them to His kingdom. It's wonderful to see people get saved, but sometimes we fear muddying the waters by talking right upfront about church membership. We don't want to complicate things from the start. But we must never forget that these new "babes in Christ" need to know how to grow in Christ.

Have you ever heard stories about newborn babies being found in things like garbage dumpsters? It breaks your heart. The young child needs a home where it can be nourished and trained to grow up.

It's the same for a newborn believer in the kingdom of God. It's a tragedy to see young believers abandoned to the wolves out there. They need a church home to grow and become strong for Christ. Therefore, we need to remember some vital things about the local New Testament church.

First, Jesus Christ positively identifies Himself with the church—not with Christianity. That may surprise you. Saul of Tarsus (later Paul) was persecuting the church, but when Jesus confronted him on the road to Damascus, He clearly said that Saul was, in truth, persecuting Him.

Second, Christ died for the church according to Ephesians 5:25.

Third, Paul was all in when it came to building up the church, according to II Timothy 2:10 and II Corinthians 11.

Fourth, Paul regarded persecuting the Church of God as his greatest sin, according to I Corinthians 15:9.

Fifth, the scriptures are clear that His supreme business in this age is the Church (See: Acts 15:13-17, Ephesians 3:20-21, 4:12, 5:25-27, Matthew 28:18-20, Revelation chapters 2 & 3).

Priority in Our Hearts

Today, we have a world filled with buildings that say "church" on the door, but they are far from authentic. Maybe they started out right. I remember when our church started decades ago in an elementary school. My dad was the pastor, and I was in my teens at the time. We complained about setting up the chairs, mopping the floor, and hauling all the stuff. But now we talk about those times as "the good old days." We were so excited when a hundred people would show up. We were willing to do almost anything to get people to Christ. We tried new things all the time.

Now, too often, we automatically think innovation is worldly compromise. When a church first gets started, there is a sense of excitement in the air. It's on fire for God, fueled with a passion for God. The people are serving, sacrificial, submissive, and strong. They are always dreaming about new ways to reach lost souls.

Then, at some point, the church finds its legs. She now has enough human resources and money to operate and keep things going. People no longer have to serve and sacrifice so much. Things shift to where people start thinking about what the church can do for them. Around this time, the passion for God's glory dwindles. It becomes directed to personal pleasure for a style of music, a favorite teacher, and preferred activities.

This is the generation that talks a lot about the good old days but forgets what made them so good. It wasn't because of a special kind of music or style of preaching; it was because there was a collective passion for God's glory more than the "felt needs" of people.

When a church gets to that point, if they're not careful, they will lose the power of God and get frustrated knowing what could be done, what has been done, but is not being done. They hope younger members will help, so they focus on that. But they only increase division over generational preferences.

If we would get our eyes off of ourselves and fall in love with God anew, we could find it refreshing. This was the message Jesus had for the church at Ephesus in the Book of Revelation.

When the Apostle John was languishing as an old man on Patmos, a prison island in the Aegean Sea, toward the end of the first century, he received a powerful revelation from God. It became the final book of the New Testament. It is filled with powerful prophecy and dramatic imagery. But the first part of what John received from Jesus was about some churches—local congregations in Proconsular Asia (modern-day Turkey). Jesus had messages for seven churches, including one at a place called Ephesus. Jesus commanded the believers there for many great qualities but issued a powerful rebuke.

> *"Unto the angel of the church of Ephesus write; These things saith he that holdeth the seven stars in his right hand, who walketh in the midst of the seven golden candlesticks; I know thy works, and thy labour, and thy patience, and how thou canst not bear them which are evil: and thou hast tried them which say they are apostles, and are not, and hast found them liars: And hast borne, and hast patience, and for my name's sake hast laboured, and hast not fainted. Nevertheless I have somewhat against thee, because thou hast left thy first love. Remember therefore from whence thou art fallen, and repent, and do the first works; or else I will come unto thee quickly, and will remove thy candlestick out of his place, except thou repent."*
>
> — Revelation 2:4-5

He told them to go back to what they had done long before—"do the things you did at first." For them to truly repent, they had to remember. What was at stake? The candlestick would be removed. What does that mean? Well, at the beginning of the passage, Jesus said he moved "in the midst of the seven golden candlesticks"—the seven local churches. Removing the candlestick meant removing their very sense of being an authentic church—it was, in essence, removing their official charter.

He told them to recover their "first love." This means to fall in love with God all over again. If we do this, God will open the windows of heaven and bless His church. The place will break open. We would see growth that wasn't the result of a marketing plan or technique. It won't even be because of a unique methodology of the past or present. It will directly result from a right and healthy relationship between the body and the head. If they're connected, the church will grow for God's glory.

I love the old *Webster's English Dictionary* because I love studying what words really mean. The word "glorify" means: "to honor, to boast, to extol, to magnify, to praise extravagantly." It means trying to make something appear as big as it really is. One definition of what it means to glorify God is to be "the best possible advertisement of all God is and does." We were created for His Glory.

A glorious church—yet another reason the church is a *big deal.*

---

[1] New Barna Survey Finds 1 in 3 Christians Stopped Attending Online or In-Person Church Services During Pandemic, Andrea Morris, CBNNews.com, July 13, 2020

CHAPTER THREE

"What's the Big Deal about the PREACHING of the Church"

Even as far back as the New Testament, believers took issue with preaching and teaching. It was boring. The preacher took too long to make his point. It was too negative, too loud, and irrelevant. Was there validity to these complaints? Is preaching necessary? Is it important? Would a brief sermonette be enough to carry us through the week? Perhaps we just need a brief devotional challenge and a longer song service.

The best way to answer any of these questions is to consider what God says about it in Scripture. In Mark 16:15, we see Jesus' final words to His church before He ascended back into glory: *"Go ye into all the world, and preach the gospel to every creature."*

Consider first of all the call to preach. From the time the New Testament church was established, preaching has been foundational. And when we think of preaching, we cannot help but think of John the Baptist. John was a bold witness for Jesus Christ. He was a man's man, coming out of the wilderness with no formal training or superficial credentials to preach to his own people about the coming of Jesus. That took real courage. The most difficult people in all the world to preach to are your family and your close friends. It's much easier to talk to strangers than it is to people who know you.

Yet John did so—because God called him to preach. John 1:6 says, *"There was a man sent from God whose name was John."* In Matthew 3:1-2, we read, *"In those days came John the Baptist preaching in the wilderness of Judea and saying repent for the kingdom of heaven is at hand."* The Bible makes it clear that John was called to preach by God. It wasn't a job; it was his God-given mission.

Jesus obeyed the call to preach. Matthew 4:23 says, *"And Jesus went about all Galilee teaching in their synagogues and preaching the gospel of the kingdom."* Wouldn't it have been awesome to hear Jesus preach? What a privilege those people were given. Mark 1:14 tells us, *"Jesus came into Galilee preaching."* Again, in Luke 8:1, we read, *"Jesus went throughout every city and village preaching."* Not only did Jesus obey the call to preach, but the disciples were likewise called to preach.

In Luke 9:1-2, we see Jesus call His twelve disciples and send them out to preach the kingdom of God and to heal the sick. Later, in verse six, we read, *"And they departed, and went through the towns, preaching the gospel, and healing everywhere."* The power of the gospel spread and others were spurred on to preach. In the Book of Acts, we read about the ministries of Steven and Philip, neither man preaching for personal fame or glory but because God had called them to do so.

Paul said preaching was more important than any other calling. Consider the ordinances of the church — baptism and communion. Preaching is more important than either of them. First Corinthians 1:17 says, *"For Christ sent me not to baptize, but to preach the gospel: not with wisdom of words, lest the cross of Christ should be made of none effect."* Paul was not diluting the value of baptism, but rather prioritizing the responsibilities of a man called to preach.

Ecclesiastes 7:2 tells us it's more important to preach than it is to attend a funeral. Jesus Himself said in Luke

9:60, "*Let the dead bury their dead: but go thou and preach the kingdom of God.*"

Jesus wasn't insensitive to those sorrowful over the loss of a loved one, but He emphasized that everyone will die someday. If we have a message to help people, we need to share the gospel before it's too late. In fact, God has put a premium on preaching. 1 Corinthians 1:21 tells us that "*it pleased God by the foolishness of preaching to save them that believe.*"

Let's pretend for a moment that we're all unsaved, just natural men and women lost in our sin. If you think back on the days before coming to faith in Christ, many of us mocked preachers. They get excited, and their faces redden as they run back and forth on the platform, looking as though they're going to explode at any minute. Who in the world would choose to have a man yell at them for an hour?

But for those of us who are saved, we understand it is the power of God unto salvation. Some would argue, "But we come to church to worship, so we should be singing, but when you have such long sermons you cut into our worship time." I would suggest to you that preaching is part of the worship service.

Martin Luther stated with Biblical accuracy that the highest worship of God is the preaching of His Word. Think about it. We as a church cannot honor God more than by listening reverently to His Word with a submissive heart. In the Old Testament, Scripture tells us that when the saints of God gathered to worship the Lord, they would stand for five or six hours. There were no padded seats, yet they listened reverently as the Word of God was read and preached, worshipping from their hearts.

They were listening as if God Himself was speaking to them.

That's our supreme act of worship. Preaching does not interrupt a worship service; preaching *is* worship because it focuses on God revealed through His Word. Preaching is important to God and true worshipers. That's why Jesus commanded us as a church to preach. In his book, *Preaching*, G. Campbell Morgan said, "The supreme work of the Christian minister is the work of preaching. This is a day in which one of our great perils is that of doing a thousand little things to the neglect of the one thing, which is preaching."

Secondly, the instruction to preach we see in Mark 16 is not a suggestion. It's a command. Remember, Jesus said, "Go ye and preach." Acts 10:42 says, "*And he commanded us to preach unto the people.*" Again, we see His command in 2 Timothy 4:1, "*I charge thee therefore before God, and the Lord Jesus Christ, who shall judge the quick and the dead at his appearing and his kingdom.*" Then in 1 Corinthians 9:16, the apostle Paul gives a personal test, "*For though I preach the gospel, I have nothing to glory of: for necessity is laid upon me; yea, woe is unto me, if I preach not the gospel!*" Though the people may have said, "Paul, that was a great message, we enjoyed your preaching today," he wanted them to know that God compelled him to preach the gospel. If he failed in His calling, he would not answer to man, but God.

Several years ago, a large church here in America was looking for a preacher. I asked the search committee about the men that they were reviewing as candidates. One man who was high on their list came with excellent organizational skills and an ability to manage finances. He was very talented and highly educated. I asked a simple question, "Can he preach?" They responded, "He's a pretty good communicator, but he is so talented in many other ways."

God calls preachers to preach. I may not be the best organizer in the world, but my primary responsibility is not organization. Say there's a light bulb out in the auditorium. Please don't come to me with a problem like that on a Sunday morning. I've got more important business.

Preachers must learn how to preach. How can a pastor expect respect or remuneration if he does not pour himself into the very thing God has called him to do, and that's to preach the Word of God? How can a missionary not be considered a con artist if he does not zealously preach? How can an evangelist overcome the charge of being a scammer if he does not preach? Those called to preach must prioritize studying and preparing themselves because that is their calling from God.

When it comes to preaching, no member should go home week after week, month after month, year after year, feeling obligated to their church yet bored out of their mind because the preacher comes to the pulpit unprepared, not having studied the Word of God. Every church member has the responsibility to preach as well. Mark 16:15, says "go ye." Now, if it were singular, speaking to one man, He would say "go thee." The specific noun used is important—"go ye" is plural, meaning that Jesus is saying every single one of you has the responsibility to preach the gospel.

What does that mean for you? Obviously, we can't all take turns in the pulpit, tag-team style as they do in wrestling, although some might find that more interesting.

The word preach means "to declare publicly, to expound or proclaim, to urge with earnestness seeking life change." The Greek word used is *kirýtto*, meaning to proclaim a victory message, a reference to the courier who would run to the town square where the people would hear important news and declarations. *Kirýtto* also means to announce, summon, decree, or demonstrate. Our actions can sometimes speak louder than our words, but that doesn't mean we shouldn't use our lives to proclaim the Word of God, but it does mean we need to demonstrate it with our life as well.

Consider Frank. He was saved and joined a local church. He worked his way into the new fellowship, not knowing the people or their personalities. He soon ran into Mildred, the church gossip, who felt God calling her to stick her nose into everybody's business. Most members disapproved of her behavior, but they were too intimidated by her to speak up.

Mildred made the mistake of approaching Frank in front of the church body. She accused him of being an alcoholic because she had seen his old pickup truck in front of the town's only bar one afternoon. "I saw your truck parked over there in front of the bar. And we all know what goes on in there. It's wrong for you to be drinking Frank, being a new member of the church and a new Christian." Frank stared at her for a moment, then simply turned and walked away. He didn't explain, he didn't defend himself, and he didn't deny it. He didn't say anything. But later that night, Frank drove over to her home and left his truck parked in her driveway. He left it there all night long.

Frank learned how to demonstrate the message.

You see, it's not just the job of the preacher to preach. That's my first and foremost priority, but every one of us that names the name of Christ has a responsibility to publicly declare the good news of Jesus Christ.

Third, consider the content of preaching. Preaching is important, but *what* we preach is equally important. As I've said throughout my ministry—it makes a difference what you believe. So often, we hear the opposite, that it doesn't make any difference what you believe, that we all believe in the same God. No. It does make a difference.

Your eternal destiny depends on what you believe. Therefore, what we preach is vital.

Paul opens his letter to the believers in Galatians with a warning about false teachers, saying there will be preachers who will come, and they'll be good communicators. They'll motivate you. They'll sound good, and perhaps they'll even quote scripture. But their preaching may be something contrary to the Word of God. Paul then offers these sobering words, *"But though we, or an angel from heaven, preach any other gospel unto you than that which we have preached unto you, let him be accursed."* That's strong language. Paul wasn't trying to be politically correct; he was being direct and truthful.

If you didn't catch it the first time, let me repeat Paul's warning. Why? Because what you believe is critically important to your eternal destiny. Think of it like this. One night, a man begins to feel ill, so he runs to the medicine cabinet, looking for the nitro pills he takes for a serious heart condition. But because it's late at night, it's dark, and he's still sleepy, he grabs the wrong bottle of medication, one containing ingredients that contradict the medication for his heart; it works like poison, and rather than save, it kills him.

You may say, "That's not fair!" He was sincere, and he simply made a mistake. Tragically, that doesn't change what poison will do in a man's body. Around the world, people are going to churches seeking a cure for their sinful disease. And they're saying, "Oh, God help me!" Yet, the false preachers are prescribing medicine that is poisoning their souls for all eternity.

Think of some of the great "preachers" in history who preached a false message. Look at Adolf Hitler. If you saw those old black and white videos, Hitler was a preaching machine. I know we look at him as a political figure and a dictator, but when you watch old films of him speaking, you see him motivate tens of thousands of men to lay down their lives for his false doctrine. Think of Joseph Stalin, Vladimir Lenin, and Louis Farrakhan.

Consider powerful orators throughout history who have captivated an audience's attention, motivating them to believe their message. Yet, it's false teaching, and those souls will be damned for all eternity.

Let me bring it closer to home. There are many TV evangelists under the umbrella of Christianity. A few years ago, one of these men said he saw 900-feet tall Jesus, and if we didn't send millions of dollars to help revive a hospital in Tulsa, God was going to take him to heaven. That man didn't get a dime from me. That message didn't come from God's Word.

Yet many Christians are deceived by this "health and wealth gospel." I know people that love the Lord Jesus and walk with God. They don't have ten cents to spend, but they're every bit as godly as the man that's rolling in dough. Your financial status has nothing to do with your salvation. We're to preach the gospel; we're to preach the cross of the Lord Jesus Christ. 2 Corinthians 10:14, says, *"For we stretch not ourselves beyond our measure, as though we reached not unto you: for we are come as far as to you also in preaching the gospel of Christ."* The word gospel means "good news." The bad news is that you're a sinner because you have sinned. You deserve to go to hell. Nobody likes to hear that, but it's a fact. The good news is that Christ came and died for your sins, for my sins, the sins of the world.

Jesus paid our debt so that anyone who puts their faith in Him can be saved from sin. Acts 11:20 says, *"when they were come to Antioch, spake unto the Grecians, preaching the Lord Jesus."* In Acts 17:3, we read, *"Opening and alleging, that Christ must needs have suffered, and risen again from the dead; and that this Jesus, whom I preach unto you, is Christ."* 1 Corinthians 1:18 promises, *"For the preaching of the cross is to them that perish foolishness; but unto us which are saved it is the power of God."*

In 2 Corinthians 4:5, Paul says, *"For we preach not ourselves, but Christ Jesus the Lord."* So, when people come to our churches, whether it be the pastor in the pulpit that morning, one of the other preachers on staff, or any visiting preacher, he is not to preach on what Baptists believe nor some creed or denominational thought. He's not even there to preach American patriotism. That man is there to preach Christ and His Word. You can be an American and yet split hell wide open when you die. You can be a Baptist and still spend eternity in hell.

But if you want to escape that, there's only one way to heaven, and that's why we preach Jesus Christ and Him alone. We are to preach repentance, meaning to change one's mind. The man that thinks that a little bit of sin is fine is lost and on his way to hell, whether he believes it or not.

As believers, we don't think as the world thinks. The world says you may need to lie, cheat, and steal to get what you want, but Acts 14:15 reminds us, *"Sirs, why do ye these things? We also are men of like passions with you, and preach unto you that ye should turn from these vanities unto the living God."* Some may say, "Well, I'll get to heaven my way." No. You'll get to heaven His way, or you won't go at all. Jesus tells us in John 14:6, *"I am the way, the truth, and the life: no man cometh unto the Father, but by me."* Note he says, "no man." Do you struggle with those two words, "no man?" That means not anybody, not even you. "No man, cometh unto the father, but by Me."

Acts 15:35 says that Paul and Barnabas continued in Antioch teaching and preaching the Word of the Lord. That's why I don't get up and preach from the newspaper or preach out of the most popular book on the market today. I'm not opposed to the newspaper or outside reading, but that's not why we go to church. We go to hear what God has to say, not man.

In 2 Timothy 4:2, Paul says to preach the Word. It makes a difference. When the church I pastor—Sauk Trail Baptist Temple—was founded more than five decades ago, church leaders put together the Articles of Faith—what we believe and what we know the scripture teaches.

Let me give an overview of those beliefs:

> *We believe in the verbal complete and total inspiration and authority of the holy scriptures. We believe in the Holy Trinity, one God eternally existing in three persons. God, the Father, God, the Son, and God, the*

Holy Spirit. We believe in the Virgin birth of Jesus Christ. We believe in Christ's death on the cross and His shed blood as the only sacrifice for sin. We believe in the bodily resurrection of Jesus Christ. We believe in the personal and imminent return of Jesus Christ. We believe in the new birth, meaning that being born again is necessary for salvation. We believe that salvation is not dependent upon works of the flesh but comes to any who, by faith, receives Jesus Christ as personal Savior. We believe in the blessed assurance and eternal security of all believers who have personally accepted Jesus Christ. We believe in two church ordinances— Baptism and the Lord's Supper. These are not a means of nor essential to salvation. We believe in followers of Christ living a separated life. We believe in tithing. We believe in soul winning. We believe in a literal Heaven and a literal hell. We believe in the bodily resurrection of the dead, the believer to everlasting blessedness and joy with the Lord, the unbeliever to judgment, and eternal conscious punishment. We believe in the separation of church and state.

A man's confession about what he believes has eternal dividends. So, when you talk to someone about God's Word and they say, "I just don't believe that," don't criticize the man. He's being honest. He doesn't believe it. Maybe he hasn't yet been drawn by the Holy Spirit to believe. Perhaps he's not yet seen the light of the gospel. So don't criticize that man, be patient and continue to witness to him, and allow the spirit of God to work in his life because you cannot make somebody believe.

There's an old expression, "You can lead a horse to water, but you can't make him drink." Likewise, you can't force someone to get saved. Our responsibility is to preach the gospel to them, let the spirit of God work in their heart, and draw them to Jesus Christ. We're not salespeople trying to get someone to jump on our bandwagon. We're ambassadors for Jesus Christ, just one beggar telling another beggar where we found bread, not higher and more important than anyone else; we're simply sharing what Jesus Christ has done for us and what He can do for them.

My father was a preacher, but I'm not going to heaven today because he was a preacher. My dad could not make me receive Jesus Christ as Savior. My wife and I had five baby girls, and sure we taught them the Word of God, but we could not make them get saved.

Rachel is our second born child. Her older sister Christina got saved when she was four or five, but Rachel was another story. Christina was a talker from the day she was born. "Hi, dad. What's the weather like?" She just came out, chatting away. Rachel was slower to speak her mind and share her thoughts, and it concerned us as parents. We'd pray and pray. We'd have family time, play games, go for walks in the woods, and slip in a bit of spelling practice. "We'd say, okay, Rachel, spell bike." "B-i-k-e." Then we'd say, "Spell saved." Do you know what she did? She got up and walked out of the room. Talk about smiting a parent's heart! Dear God, what have we done wrong? She doesn't even want to hear the word "saved!"

But, as dad and mom, we could not make our children trust Christ. We could simply preach the gospel to them and pray for the Holy Spirit to work in their heart to receive Jesus Christ as Lord and Savior of their own volition. If I can talk them into being saved, some other person can come and talk them out of it.

The Bible says in Romans 10:10, *"For with the heart man believeth unto righteousness; and with the mouth confession is made unto salvation."* So, when a man gets saved, it's because he's responding to the Holy Spirit moving in him powerfully.

There must be consistency in our preaching. Matthew 28:19-20 says, *"Go ye therefore, and teach all nations, baptizing them in the name of the Father, and of the*

Son, and of the Holy Ghost: Teaching them to observe all things whatsoever I have commanded you: and, lo, I am with you always, even unto the end of the world." God commands us to preach and teach the gospel to all nations, but the message is the same to all—salvation by faith in Christ alone.

Church growth seminars can teach you how to market to certain people. If you want to reach lower-income people, use this method. If you wish to attract the wealthy, use another way. Some will say if you're going to be a successful preacher, you need to choose which kind of people you want to target so that you can market to them effectively, or you'll never grow a megachurch. I'm not going to question their motives, but I'm here to tell you that's not important to me.

Whether you have $10 million in your pocket or if you have ten cents, the gospel is important to both of you. One will go to hell with ten cents in his pocket; the other will go to hell with $10 million in his pocket. Money does not affect your eternal destiny. In fact, the more money you have, the less likely you are to get saved because it will be more difficult for you to let go of what you have to trust in God.

We're to be consistent. We don't single out a certain group of people that we want to reach. We're to preach the gospel to everyone. For example, some churches want to appeal to young people, so they change the music to be more appealing while others stick with hymns. Some churches offer traditional and contemporary services to appeal to both crowds. I'm here to tell you that if it's Bible music, the young and the old may have to learn it, but they're going to like it because it lifts the name of Jesus Christ. Even when people move from one Baptist church to another, they have to learn new music because no two Baptist churches are alike. Thank God He is consistent.

We're to be faithful in preaching to everyone, everywhere, all the time. Matthew 10:27 challenges us, *"What I tell you in darkness, that speak ye in light: and what ye hear in the ear, that preach ye upon the housetops."* Acts 8:4 tells us, *"Therefore they, that were scattered abroad, went everywhere, preaching the Word again,"* and in 2 Timothy 4:2, Paul commands us to *"Preach the word; be instant in season, out of season; reprove, rebuke, exhort with all longsuffering and doctrine."* That simply means we're to preach when people like it when they don't like it, when it's popular, when it's unpopular, because the fact is, most people don't want to hear it.

Very few times in my ministry have I had anyone call me and say, "What must I do to be saved?" though it has happened. Years ago, a young couple was going through a difficult time in their lives, so they reached out to me. I was in the old sound room in the back in the auditorium and picked up the phone. This lady started pouring out her heart. So, I simply presented the gospel to her. She trusted Christ as Savior right on there on the phone.

When I hung up, I thought perhaps she was just emotionally charged. Nobody gets saved on the phone. I'd never had someone call me and say, "Hey, what do I need to do to get saved?" Because she had given me her address, I visited her, and I led her husband to the Lord as well. Both of them were faithful members at our church until he passed away and she moved away.

When someone inquires, "What must I do to be saved," it is because someone went before me and told them about Jesus Christ. Most of the world does not want to hear the gospel. Not every generation is as open to the Word of God. Not every culture is tolerant of the Bible, but that does not excuse us from being consistent. We are to preach the gospel. We are to preach repentance. We are to preach the Word of God, no matter what people might say.

And that kind of preaching is part of what makes the church a big deal.

CHAPTER FOUR

"What's the Big Deal about the PICTURES of the Church?"

It has been said that a picture is worth a thousand words. For nearly 50 years I've carried a picture of my bride. There have been times when we were out of sorts, and I was upset with her. I would get alone and think. Sometimes I would not have very good thoughts. Then I would open my wallet, look at her picture, and remember the fun dating years we had. The first time I saw her smile. When she walked down the aisle. Getting her into our little 1973 yellow *Volkswagon Super Beetle* and heading off to our honeymoon destination.

I remember the Wagon Wheel, a great honeymoon resort, in Rockton, IL. And, of course, I remember the five baby girls she gave me, and trained to love and respect me. Soon, my heart is softened, and I remember why I love her so much.

It is just one picture—but it has power to change my heart's attitude.

It's like the story of the nice calm and respectable lady who went into a pharmacy. She looked straight into the eyes of the pharmacist and said, "I would like to buy some cyanide."

The pharmacist asked, "Why do you need cyanide?"

"I need it to poison my husband," she replied.

The pharmacist's eyes got very large as he exclaimed, "I can't give you cyanide to kill your husband. That's against the law. I would lose my license. They will throw both of us in jail. All kinds of bad things will happen. Absolutely not. You cannot have any cyanide!"

The woman reached into her purse and pulled out a picture of her husband at a fancy restaurant, having dinner with the pharmacist's wife. The pharmacist looked at the picture and replied, "Now that's different. You didn't say you had a prescription."

Pictures can make a difference. Just one of them can change our whole thought process. The two pictures in the church can literally change our hearts and help us to fall in love with our Savior all over again. You see, God knows how capable we are of forgetting good things. He knows that we can have a great respect and value something today, but then—in time—think of it less and less.

What's the big deal about church? Well, it's a big deal to God. People sometimes fail to appreciate something because they know so little about it. Jesus started His church. He empowered the church. He meets with the church. He died for it. He is preparing a place for it. He loves the church and is glorified in the church. Therefore, anyone who truly loves Jesus loves His church.

Period.

It is also true that we can have a great respect and even value something today, and then over time forget it and fail to appreciate it. So, we need to be reminded about it from time to time in order to appreciate its value.

I want to point out to you two *pictures* of the church that will help us appreciate the entrance into the church. I am referring to two pictures that the Lord Jesus Christ used to describe His church.

The first picture is *baptism*. 1 Peter 3:21 says, *"The like figure whereunto even baptism doth also now save us (not the putting away of the filth of the flesh, but the answer of a good conscience toward God), by the resurrection of Jesus*

Christ." If you only read part of that verse, it would seem like it is saying that baptism saves us. And, for those who believe in baptismal regeneration, they use this portion of scripture to "prove" that baptism does save us. But look at the words, "like figure." We see God is speaking *allegorically*—that's what "figure" means. It's a picture. If you read this verse in its full context, the author is giving us an illustration referring back to the days of Noah.

Those who were in the Ark were saved because of their faith and belief and trust in God. The ark itself did not save them. When a man believes, it is not just an emotional feeling, but it comes out in his lifestyle. It is an obedience as shown in God's Word.

Peter was saying that just like in the days of Noah, baptism does now also save us. People get saved—then they get baptized. Why? Because it is God's command. Baptism puts the ring on the finger and lets the world know that someone believes in and belongs to Jesus Christ.

He didn't want you to err from the truth, so Peter inserted a parenthetical thought: *"Not putting away of the filth of the flesh, but the answer of a good conscience toward God."* He is reminding us and reinforcing the truth that baptism cannot actually wash away sin. You could get dunked 50 times, but if you're not saved, you'd still die in your sins.

Baptism doesn't wash away our sins. The blood of Jesus Christ cleanses us from our sins. Baptism is simply a picture. It's a "like figure" of the fact that we have believed in the death, burial, and resurrection of Jesus Christ. That's why when we baptize, we don't just refer to the Lord's death. We bury in the likeness of His death—but that's not the whole story. We bring them up out of the water—in the likeness of His resurrection.

The second picture comes from 1 Corinthians 11:26: *"For as often as ye eat this bread, and drink this cup, ye do show the Lord's death till he come."* The second picture is the *Lord's Supper*. We remember Christ's death. These two pictures are the two ordinances that Jesus instructs us to observe in His church. Baptism and the Lord's Supper.

These two ordinances hold no supernatural magical powers in and of themselves. These pictures cannot save you. Baptism doesn't save you. Partaking in the Lord's Supper does not save you.

Of course, I have many friends in the Roman Catholic church who believe differently. When I point out the differences of the Bible and other church doctrine, I am not criticizing them. I am simply informing my readers about what the Bible says, so they can decide for yourself.

The Roman Catholicism teaches both baptismal regeneration and infant baptism. I don't believe in infant baptism. An infant is not capable of understanding what is happening. He is not deciding that he wants to follow Christ. Parents cannot force babies into the family of God. That is impossible. Nobody can be saved for someone else. And baptism doesn't put anyone into the family of God.

Many Protestant Churches also practice infant baptism, and in their doctrinal statement they believe that it puts them into the family of God. Then, at the age of 11 or 12 or 13, they have a ritual that they call *confirmation*. Confirmation is when a child who was baptized into the family of God, is indeed in the family of God. They confirm that they believe and will follow Christ.

But according to the Bible, all that they are confirming with that child is contradictory to the teaching of God's Word. A man doesn't need to be confirmed. He needs to be born again. A man doesn't need to be baptized. He needs to be immersed into God's love and learn of Jesus Christ, who died for his sins, was buried, and rose again from the grave. He needs to, by faith, receive Christ as Lord and Savior.

I'm not condemning these other churches. I'm just simply pointing out that there's a huge difference of opinion about these two pictures. These pictures are to bring to remembrance precious memories of events that took place that have radically changed our lives.

Consider the first picture—Baptism

Colossians 2:12 says, *"Buried with him in baptism, wherein also ye are rinse with him through the faith of the operation of God, who hath raised him from the dead." Roman 6:4 says, "Therefore, we are buried with him by baptism into death: that like as Christ was raised up from the dead by the glory of the father, even so we also should walk in newness of life."*

We should walk in newness of life. Baptism is a picture of a new life in Jesus Christ. It is an act of obedience to the Lord. Acts 2:38 says, *"Repent and be Baptized every one of you in the name of Jesus Christ for the remission of sins."* The word, "for," in that verse, means *because of.*

Baptism also follows the example of the Lord. Mark 1:9 says, *"And it came to pass in those days that Jesus came from Nazareth of Galilee, and was baptized of John in*

Jordan." In fact, Jesus walked 69 miles from Nazareth to the Jordan river to be baptized. That's how important baptism was to Him. And because it was important to Jesus, it should be important to us.

Remember the day you decided to ask Jesus into your heart? There was a joy unspeakable in your heart and you wanted to reciprocate somehow. God didn't ask you to build something with your hands or to give money to the church. He asked you to humble yourself so that you could respond to God with gratitude for His salvation. We humble ourselves by letting someone put us in the water and bring us back out. Baptism is an answer of a good conscience toward God.

Baptism is also the door into the church. 1 Corinthians 12:13 says, *"For by one spirit, we were all baptized into one body..."*—the body of Christ is His Church. Baptism is an outward expression of an inward experience.

Four Biblical Requirements for Baptism

First, there must be the *right candidate.* The person baptized must be saved. (Therefore, not a baby.) When we baptize someone, we ask that person if they know Jesus Christ as their personal Savior. Why? Because it is important and it is what scripture commands. They must understand their need for Christ because of their sin. They must acknowledge the fact that the spirit of God is drawing them to salvation. So, they call upon the name of the Lord and are saved. Whether they are five-years-old, or 105-years-old, there is a joy in their heart and desire to be obedient to the Lord.

Sometimes we see people who were baptized in a Baptist Church, but they later realize that they weren't truly saved. So, they asked Jesus into their heart and then were re-baptized. Why did they need to be baptized again? Because their first baptism was not Biblical, because they weren't truly saved.

Paul faced this situation in Acts chapter 19. He came across some disciples having a conversation about church life and doctrine. Paul discerned that they did not sound like they were truly saved. They didn't understand what the gospel was about. So, he probed a little, and he discovered that they had never even heard of the Holy Spirit. So he preached Christ to them. They believed and were baptized.

Baptism *always* follows salvation.

The second requirement for baptism is the candidate needs to have the *right motive*. That motive is obedience.

It's not for salvation. We get baptized simply to obey God.

Can someone go to heaven if they have not been baptized? Absolutely. But they will be embarrassed at the Judgment Seat of Christ. Not being baptized is disobedience to the Lord. You cannot be a disobedient child of God and expect the full blessings of God.

Dr. Harry Ironside, the great Bible teacher and writer, said, "an unbaptized believer is a contradiction of terms." He was right. It is an oxymoron. Because people who have a new nature because of salvation also have a desire to be obedient to God. There should be a burning passion in the heart to obey God.

The third requirement for baptism is the *right mode*. A mode is a method. I'm speaking of immersion, versus sprinkling or pouring. The meaning of the word, "baptize" is to dip under water. The Greek word, *"baptizo"* means to immerse or dip under the water. Immersion best symbolizes the death, burial, and resurrection of Jesus Christ.

When I was a youth pastor, we would often take our five kids on a camping vacation in Wisconsin. On one visit, my wife's uncle introduced me to a Primitive Methodist preacher. He was an elderly man, and he was very kind and gracious to me, asking me if I would like to speak at his church on a Wednesday night. I was thrilled and shocked that a Methodist would ask a Baptist to preach. We chatted a bit. I asked him to tell me the difference between primitive Methodists and Baptists. He told me that there was essentially no difference between what we believe. He listed all the doctrinal statements of his church.

The only difference was in the method of baptism.

In the Primitive Methodist church, people were given the option of how they wanted to be baptized—sprinkling, pouring, or immersion. I asked him why they are given the option. He replied that it depends on what they want to represent with the baptism. The sprinkled water represents the sprinkling of the blood on the mercy seat. The pouring of the water on one's head represents the pouring of God's Spirit on mankind. Immersion represented the death, burial, and resurrection of Christ.

Of course, being a young man and quick to speak like Peter, I asked him why there needed to be a discussion about it. If the Bible says that baptism is to portray the death, burial, and resurrection, then why would he give the people choices? He smiled very calmly and told me that he agreed with me. He told me that it was the denominational stand. He had to offer the choices, but personally believed the Bible teaches that immersion is the proper mode for baptism. Praise the Lord for that.

Do you realize that the Protestant churches today that practice sprinkling and pouring are actually contradicting the founders of their own churches?

Martin Luther, founder of the Lutheran church said, "I would have those who are to be baptized, to be entirely immersed as the word imports and the mystery signifies."

John Calvin, who is the founder of the Presbyterian church, said, "The word baptize signifies to immerse. It is certain that immersion was the practice of the ancient church."

John Wesley, founder of the Methodist church said, "Buried with him eludes to baptizing by immersion according to the custom of the first church."

Jesus was baptized by immersion. Matthew 3:16 says, *"And Jesus, when he was baptized, went up straightway out of the water: and lo, the heavens were opened unto him, and he saw the Spirit of God descending like a dove, and lighting upon him."*

The bottom line is, every baptism in the Bible was done by immersion.

Acts 8:38-39 says, *"And he commanded the chariot to stand still; and they went down both into the water, both Philip and the eunuch; and he baptized him. And when they were come up out of the water, the Spirit of the Lord caught away Philip, that the eunuch saw him no more and he went on his way rejoicing."*

The fourth requirement for baptism is the right administrator. The administrator is the church, not individuals. Our oldest daughter, Christina, had the joy of leading some of her friends to Christ over the years. She would bring them over to our house. In our backyard, we had an above ground swimming pool. One day I looked out the back window and Christie was in the pool with her friends, saying the name of the Father, and the Son, and the Holy Ghost. I sat and smiled, and thought that it was a nice gesture.

But to be Biblically baptized, it had to be done by someone other than Christina. She did not have the authority to do that. Because the authority lies in the church.

The command, the ordinance, of baptism is not given to a denomination, a man, or a social organization.

It is given to His Church. Matthew 38:18-19 says, "*And Jesus came and spoke unto them, saying, All power is given unto me in heaven and in earth. Go ye therefore and teach all nations, baptizing them in the name of the Father, and of the Son, and of the Holy Ghost.*"

The church authorizes the pastor to minister the ordinances of the Church. But it is the church who holds the authority. If the pastor has to leave the church, then he should not administer the ordinances of the church. The authority does not lie in a man—it lies in the church. The authority was given to Jesus Christ, and then He authorized His church to go into all the world, preach the gospel, and baptize them.

It is very important to know how to pick the right church for you. You can identify a church that Jesus started by doctrine and practice. Baptism portrays the death, burial, and the resurrection of Jesus Christ. That's the gospel. The good news for lost sinners. Baptism reminds us of that good news.

The Picture of the Lord's Supper

This second ordinance is sometimes called *communion.* God realizes how quickly we forget, and therefore He has given us baptism and the Lord's Supper to help us

A fourth way to prepare for the Lord's Supper is to do our part to restore broken relationships. Matthew 5:23-24 says, *"Therefore if thou bring thy gift to the altar, and there remember that thy brother hath ought against thee; Leave there thy gift before the altar, and go thy way; first be reconciled to thy brother, and then come and offer thy gift."*

When should we observe the Lord's supper?

1 Corinthians 11:26 says, *"For as often as ye eat this bread, and drink this cup, ye do show the Lord's death till he come."*

While Scripture tells us what to do to prepare for it, Jesus never told us how often believers should observe the Lord's Supper. Some churches observe it weekly. Some observe it monthly. Some, quarterly.

In my church, we observe the Lord's Supper once per year, on the Tuesday night before Easter. Why do we do that? Do you remember when Jesus instituted this ordinance? It was on the eve of His crucifixion. Jesus and the disciples were observing Passover, to remember how the Death Angel passed over every home that had the blood of the lamb applied on their door in Egypt. That was the action that set the Israelites free from bondage and slavery. The Jewish people still practice it today.

However, Jesus instituted something NEW and established a New covenant, a New Testament covenant, with true believers.

The elements He used were bread and wine (a cup of grape juice, not fermented wine). We see the difference between new wine and old wine, the fruit of the vine, in Matthew 26:29. The bread represents His body, broken for us. And the wine represents His blood, shed for us.

Jesus did this on the eve of His death, so it was likely on a Tuesday, as Christ was likely crucified on Wednesday. The Passover was observed once a year, so there is a Biblical case for observing the Lord's Supper on the Tuesday before Easter.

Matthew 12:40 says, *"For as Jonah was three days and three nights in the whale's belly; so shall the Son of man be three days and three nights in the heart of the earth."*

The two pictures the Lord has asked the church to display are Baptism and the Lord's Supper. And both of them are precious pictures to those of us who are saved. These pictures prove the fact that the church is, indeed, a big deal.

CHAPTER FIVE

"What's the Big Deal about PICKING the RIGHT CHURCH?"

If you're a student of the Word of God, you're very familiar with the importance of the second chapter of the Book of Acts. Its significance can't be overstated. It records the miraculous events of the disciples being filled with the Holy Spirit's gifting, enabling each man to speak in different known languages, and to minister to those in Jerusalem celebrating the Feast of Pentecost. Some scholars estimate that more than 100,000 travelers had made the pilgrimage. Three thousand souls trusted Christ as Savior and were baptized. That day stands as one of the highlights in Christian history.

The Bible tells us Peter spoke with boldness. He chastised the crowd, telling them they were guilty of the death of Christ because of their cold hearts. Yet, Christ died for them. Acts 2:42-47 tells us:

> *"And they continued steadfastly in the apostles' doctrine and fellowship, and in breaking of bread, and in prayers. And fear came upon every soul: and many wonders and signs were done by the apostles. And all that believed were together, and had all things common; And sold their possessions and goods, and parted them to all men, as every man had need. And they, continuing daily with one accord in the temple, and breaking bread from house to house, did eat their meat with gladness and singleness of heart, Praising God, and having favor with all the people. And the Lord added to the church daily such as should be saved."*

Notice carefully, seven words in Acts 2:47, *"and the Lord added to the church."* Choosing a church is nothing to be taken lightly. As followers of Christ, we should consider several factors when we choose which church to join.

If we want to join a church with the Lord's approval, we must, first of all, be saved. Second, we must be scripturally baptized, and third, we must be striving to live a godly life. Church membership is important to God, so it must also be important to the believer in Him.

When someone approaches me about church membership, I ask several questions. "Are you saved? Have you been baptized in a Baptist church? Are you striving to live a godly life? Have you prayed about this matter? Do you believe it to be God's will to join here?" Do you know why I ask so many questions? Not so I can build a megachurch—though I'd love to have a thousand members. No—I ask so that the glory of God will be declared to more people and to have a powerful testimony of God's work here in our city.

However, I'm not looking for a crowd. God has called me to pastor a church, and that's different from simply drawing a crowd. Following the example in Acts chapter two, God's people were added to the church following His leading. So, the Lord adds to the church—not man, not the pastor, not the programs—it is His power at work.

I want to challenge you to consider something. At some point in our lives, God will lead many of us to move to another town or city. Perhaps it's a job opportunity, retirement, or a chance to move closer to family. Whatever the reason, you will be starting over in a new place. As you take that step, I encourage you to carefully consider what you should look for when choosing your new church. I would encourage you to pick out the church before you move. Your spiritual health is far more important than your home or even your place of employment. Keep God first and seek His leading in choosing.

We have a responsibility to be the kind of church God has called us to be. So, I challenge you to live as if the whole church depended upon *you*—not the preacher, not the youth director, not the choir. God placed you in your church, did He not? And if He placed you, He has a purpose for you. He wants each of us to do our part to be the church God has called us to be. But, of course, there are no perfect churches because they are filled with imperfect people. In fact, if you find a perfect church, don't join it; you'll ruin it.

Though there are no perfect churches, every Christian should be baptized and added to a local New Testament church where Jesus Christ is the head. Let me give you four reasons why you ought to join a church.

Number one, it's biblical. Do we need any other reason? If God said to be baptized and added to the local church, that ought to settle any discussion or questions that we might have. Hebrews 10:25 says, *"Not forsaking the assembling of ourselves together, as the manner of some is;*

but exhorting one another: and so much the more, as ye see the day approaching." God speaks through Paul, reminding us that though there are some out there who aren't faithful to church, that ought not to be said of you. You ought to be faithful.

There's little commitment in our culture today. However, when we commit to our local church, we must say, "I'm going to join that church. I'm going to be a part of that church family. I'm going to swim against the tide of our culture." There may be Sundays you'll think, "Wow, I didn't get anything out of the message today. But I'm part of it. I am committed. I'm obedient to what God has called me to do." Remember, every member God brings to our local churches is essential because God placed them within that church body.

If—God forbid—I accidentally sever my finger, and go to the hospital, and the doctor reattaches it, I have a good chance that, once it heals, the finger will function again. But if I sever my finger and do nothing, the tissue will wither and die. So it is with those that get saved yet never join a church—their spiritual life withers and dies. Now, they may talk a good game, and there might be some life at first, but until they join a church, they cannot grow to glorify God as He intended.

When seeking a church home, above all else, we should look for a church where the Bible is preached. The Bible is the final authority for the church, and any man who suggests otherwise is not of God. We're here to hear what God has to say, not for any man's opinion or interpretation. Open God's word, read it, teach it. That's what God's people crave, that's what the people of God hunger for, and that's what we're commanded to do in Matthew 28:18-20.

Preach the gospel.

Where you place your faith and trust makes a difference because your doctrine determines your destiny. Romans 10:10 tells us, *"For with the heart man believeth unto righteousness; and with the mouth, confession is made unto salvation."* Some may say it makes no difference what you believe because, in the end, we all believe the same thing. That's not true. Throughout the history of mankind, men have gone to war because their beliefs were wildly different. We do not all believe the same thing, nor do we worship the same God. The Bible tells us that all have sinned, but the Bible also tells us that we have a savior. Scripture is clear that we have no hope in and of ourselves, but it also tells us that God is our helper in time of need.

We don't belong to a denomination. A denomination has headquarters somewhere and they dictate to their churches how and what ought to be preached. And sometimes that's good. They govern the schools, their theological seminaries, and will also dictate what will be taught to the students. They may encourage certain kinds of giving. They also will move pastors from pulpit to pulpit. They will move preachers that are good preachers, up a notch and up a notch to where he is finally on a platform of a huge church because of his giftedness in preaching the word of God. I'm not opposed to the mechanics of all that stuff, and I'm not even judging them. I just don't find any scripture to support it. Every church should be autonomous.

Bible preaching always has Jesus Christ as its foundation. If a church truly loves the Lord Jesus Christ, His name will be lifted above all else. He'll be praised. He'll be glorified. The pastor will preach salvation through Christ alone because He alone atoned for our sin at Calvary. Acts 4:14 tells us, *"Neither is there salvation in any other: for there is none other name under heaven given among men, whereby we must be saved."*

Look for a church where the spirit is pleasant. 1 Samuel 16:7 says, *"But the LORD said unto Samuel, Look not on his countenance, or on the height of his stature; because I have refused him: for the LORD seeth not as man seeth; for man looketh on the outward appearance, but the LORD looketh on the heart."* In Proverbs 17:3, we read, *"The fining pot is for silver, and the furnace for gold: but the LORD trieth the hearts."* Matthew 9:4 says, *"And Jesus knowing their thoughts said, 'Wherefore think ye evil in your hearts?'"*

Your attitude is just as important as your actions. Often, people with bad attitudes will fill their lives with busywork and activity to deflect criticism from others, but the truth of the matter is that God looks on the heart. He knows your heart and He discerns your motives. 1 Samuel 16:7 cautions us, *"man looketh on the outward appearance, but the LORD looketh on the heart."*

Churches must be intentional in building a culture of unity. Ephesians 4:3 challenges us to endeavor to keep the unity of the Spirit in the bond of peace. The church is filled with diverse personalities, cultures, problems, and levels of spiritual maturity. Yet, with this diversity, we have unity within our church body. That's not an accident. People choose to rise above the petty things of this world to keep the main thing, the main thing—Jesus Christ above all. We rise above. That doesn't mean there is no conflict, but praise God, when Christ is the center, "the things of earth grow strangely dim in the light of His glory and grace."

It's dangerous to stir up division within the church. Romans 16:17 warns us, *"Now I beseech you, brethren, mark them which cause divisions and offences contrary to the doctrine which ye have learned; and avoid them."* We must maintain the spirit of charity. Paul emphasizes the importance of charity in 1 Corinthians 13:1, saying, *"Though I speak with the tongues of men and of angels, and have not charity, I am become as sounding brass, or a tinkling cymbal."*

We cannot please God without charity.

You can tithe; you can give to faith promise, the building project, and missions. You can be a Sunday school teacher, a choir member, and serve as a deacon, but it's worthless if you don't have charity. God says, if I don't have charity, I'm like sounding brass or tinkling cymbals. Without charity, I am nothing.

Later, in verse three it says, *"And though I bestow all my goods to feed the poor, and though I give my body to be burned, and have not charity, it profiteth me nothing."* Charity is love motivated by grace. Mark it down. When a church has charity, it's a whole lot easier to maintain unity.

We need a spirit of submission and servanthood. The Bible says in Ephesians 5:21 that we are to submit one to another in the fear of God. God placed you in a local church to minister to others. Our attitude should be, "Dear God, you placed me here. I'm willing to serve You because of all you have done for me."

The pastors and staff of a church should have a servant's heart. On Sunday mornings, I go to our church early, before most others arrive. I pray in the auditorium and throughout the church building and I'm reminded of different people, their spiritual gifts, what they do in the church, and I pray for them.

Occasionally, I'll see something missed by the cleaners or something that needs to be taken care of before services. Perhaps the person responsible got sick. Maybe they had a family issue to deal with—sometimes people just forget. So, when I find a carpet that hasn't been vacuumed or a toilet that wasn't cleaned, I don't wait until I'm in the pulpit to rebuke someone. I either do it myself or gather the other pastors and say, "We got a job to do." If you came to pray, pray, standing up. If you came to prepare your sermon, preach it to the vacuum cleaner. We are all called to serve.

We ought to have a forgiving spirit. Ephesians 4:32 says, *"And be kind one to another tenderhearted forgiving one another. Even as God for Christ's sake has forgiven you."* Forgiveness keeps you from becoming bitter. Forgiveness keeps you from being angry. Forgiveness keeps you from getting lost in your feelings.

Becoming a follower of Christ doesn't protect you from disappointment or hurt. Somebody is going to offend you. It may be a family member, a friend, or another believer. There's a good chance that your pastor may offend you. He's human, and humans are sinful, broken creatures. That's why it's vitally important that we learn to forgive one another as God forgives. 1 John 1:9 reminds us, *"If we confess our sins, he is faithful and just to forgive us our sins, and to cleanse us from all unrighteousness."*

All He asks is that we repent. God forgives the sins we mention in our prayers and even the sins we overlook. You've likely failed the Lord in many more ways than what you confessed in your prayers this morning. But God forgives all of it because of your repentance—He sees your heart.

We ought to learn to forgive one another, even as God, for Christ's sake, has forgiven us. But if you can't get over it, you owe it to that person to go to them. If I offend you, you ought to confront me and allow me to explain myself so I can make it right. Allowing resentment to fester is not the intention of someone trying to serve the Lord. Learn to forgive.

We need a spirit of joy, for the joy of the Lord is our strength. Joy is not something based on circumstances—a joyful heart is a choice. If you get a raise in pay this week, you're going to be happy, but if you get fired this week, you can still be content. The joy of the Lord is part of the fruit of the holy spirit of God. It all depends on your focus. Remember, "Turn your eyes upon Jesus, look full in His wonderful face, and the things of this world will grow strangely dim in the light of his glory and grace."

When searching for a church home, be sure to look for a church where soul winning is promoted. We're here to be a soul-saving station. Soul-winning demonstrates wisdom which is the application of knowledge. A man may exhibit an understanding of the Scriptures, but he is not showing wisdom if he's not bringing souls to Jesus Christ. His great vocabulary and ability to communicate and preach may be impressive, but he is not wise if he isn't leading men and women to Christ. Proverbs 11:30 says, *"And he that wineth souls is wise."* Soul winning brings joy both to a saint's heart and to God's heart. Psalm 126:6 tells us, *"He that goeth forth and weepeth, bearing precious seed, shall doubtless come again with rejoicing, bringing his sheaves with him."*

There is joy in leading another soul to Jesus Christ. Some may win more souls than others, but every one of us can rejoice when a soul is saved. That's what happens in heaven. Luke 15:10 says, *"Likewise, I say unto you, there is joy in the presence of the angels of God over one sinner that repenteth."* The angels didn't win that man to Christ, yet they are thrilled because that's the heart of God to see sinners converted.

Another important characteristic to look for is a church where separation is practiced. Romans 12:1-2 says, *"I beseech you therefore brethren by the mercies of God that you present your bodies, a living sacrifice holy acceptable unto God, which is your reasonable service and be not conformed to this world, but be transformed by the renewing of your mind that ye may prove what is that good and acceptable and perfect will of God."*

What is separation? On a personal level, it's when God's people separate themselves from a sinful lifestyle. Unfortunately, we've heard a lot of opinions and not biblical instruction over the last several years, and we're reaping the harvest of that today.

If a man has hair over his ear, that doesn't mean that he is lost. If a woman wears pants, it doesn't mean that she is lost, nor does it mean she is immoral, but that's what was preached years ago. I heard it with my own ears many times. Now I would suggest that a man ought to cut his hair. Some of the men that preached the hardest about long hair on men had hair that would go down to their shoulders, but they wrapped it around their head 45 times, had hairspray and a hairdryer to lacquer it in place. It looked like cotton candy on their head, but that man was considered spiritual because it didn't touch his ears.

Deuteronomy 22:5 tells us that, *"The woman shall not wear that which pertaineth unto a man, neither shall a man put on a woman's garment: for all that do so are an abomination unto the Lord thy God."* Even the world knows men and women should wear different types of clothing. For example, even if you can't read English or Spanish, you know which bathroom to use when you go to the airport. One door has a picture of a man, and the other is a woman's character in a dress. So, if you get mad at the preacher, you'll also need to get angry at the airport. Now bear in mind, you can wear a dress and still be immodest, so it's more than whether it's a dress or slacks. The issue is modesty, something the Bible is clear about.

It's more than just the way we dress, it's the entertainment we consume as well. How many of us are viewing content on television today that years ago we would never have watched? When did our standards drop? Did God change, or did you change? Why were you so strict with your kids, yet today it's okay for you to watch inappropriate programs? See, we're good at telling other people how to live, but practicing it ourselves is a whole different matter. The truth of the matter is, every church is to challenge people to live a holy, set apart life. The church should never be a haven of rest for a man that wants to live a sinful lifestyle.

We must be willing to work with those struggling so we can help them grow spiritually. If a man deliberately chooses to live contrary to the Word of God, we are commanded to approach him, to try and restore him. And if he will not repent, we should ask him to leave. Why? Because God gets no glory in our sinful activity, and the church is to be a place where God is glorified.

Now, are any of us perfect? No, but every one of us ought to be able to look another believer in the eye and say, "I am striving to live a godly life. If I fail, call me on the carpet because I want to do what's right."

In 2 Corinthians 6:17, God said, *"Wherefore come out from among them, and be ye separate, saith the Lord, and touch not the unclean thing; and I will receive you."* If I were looking for a church today, this is what I would be searching for. Your church ought to be a place where the scriptures are preached, where the spirit is pleasant, where soul-winning is promoted, and where separation is practiced.

Finally, one should search for a church where singing is plentiful. The largest book in our Bible is the book of Psalms—a hymnal. Just as much as missions is the life of the church, music is the life of the church service. If your music is dead, your services will likely be dead. Music is not just there to fill time until the preaching starts. It's not a filler. It's an essential part of the worship service. In fact, there are more references to music and the worship service in the Old Testament than that of preaching or teaching. I cannot exaggerate the importance of music in the church.

Music is a universal language. Music speaks. Jesus said, *"Out of the abundance of the heart, the mouth speaks"*

(Luke 6:45). Music has a direct effect on a man, physically, mentally, and spiritually.

In 1 Samuel 16, King Saul was suffering from a nervous breakdown resulting from demonic powers. Instead of sending for a magician, soothsayer, or a doctor, as was the custom of that time, he called for a young man named David and asked him to play his harp. After David had played a while, the Bible says, *"And it came to pass, when the evil spirit from God was upon Saul, that David took a harp, and played with his hand: So Saul was refreshed, and was well, and the evil spirit departed from him."* David's music refreshed Saul's spirit, and the evil spirit left him. That's why it's so vital that choose with care the kind of music you listen to.

The music we listen to today is detrimental to the average person's health, let alone his spiritual well-being. Some people worship their music. We usually associate that behavior with teenagers, but they aren't the only ones who are guilty. When my wife and I traveled to Maui, we visited a remote community called Hāna. It's a beautiful journey, but you can't drive more than 10-15 miles an hour because the curves are so sharp. Before you get onto those narrow little roads, you pass through a town filled with Baby Boomers who came out of the seventies yet never grew up. They're still wearing tie-dye t-shirts and the same bell-bottoms that they had back then. This community of people worship the music of their era. These aren't children; they're men and women my age, yet they are obsessed with their music.

Did you know that attitude creeps into the church too?

For years, we've had division in the church over styles of music because people worship their music. They forget what music is all about. Music is intended to draw our hearts to God and to praise Him. Of course, there is much debate over what "worldly" music is. Just because it isn't your style or preference doesn't make it worldly, but there are music styles that have hurt many churches today. A church should be filled with music.

Scripture commands us to sing. Colossians 3:16 says, *"Let the word of Christ dwell in you richly in all wisdom; teaching and admonishing one another in psalms and hymns and spiritual songs, singing with grace in your hearts to the Lord."* When Moses and the children of Israel crossed into the promised land, they sang because of their redemption. Jesus Himself sang a hymn with His disciples just before His crucifixion. While they were in jail, Paul and Silas sang a song, blessed the heart of God, and God shook the earth and set them free. In Revelation 5, we read that there's going to be great singing in heaven. It's one of the primary means by which everyone will participate in worshipping God. Not everybody can play the piano, trumpet, or violin, and not everyone can sing a solo, but we can all sing aloud in our congregational singing. It prepares the heart of people for the message to follow.

When people sing to the Lord, they prepare themselves to hear from the Lord. *"O sing unto the Lord a new song: sing unto the Lord, all the earth. Sing unto the Lord, bless his name; shew forth his salvation from day to day. Declare his glory among the heathen, his wonders among all people. For the Lord is great, and greatly to be praised: he is to be feared above all gods. O sing unto the Lord, a new song, sing unto the Lord. All the earth sing unto the Lord. Bless his name. Show forth his salvation from day to day, declare his glory among the heathen. His wonders among all people for the Lord is great and greatly to be praised. He is to be feared above all gods."* (Psalm 96:1-4).

Psalm 95 tells us, *"Oh, come let us sing them to the Lord. Let us make a joyful noise to the rock of our salvation."* That command is there for all those who can't sing.

We're commanded to sing, and for those who can't, He says to make a joyful noise.

I want to challenge you. If your church depended on you, just, you, ask yourself, "Do I preach the scriptures to every creature" Do I have a pleasant spirit? Do I promote soul-winning? Do I practice separation? Do I participate in singing? Someone with a defeatist attitude would say, "Oh, he's just trying to get me to leave my church or make me feel guilty." No, but I am asking you to examine your heart and see if you are obedient to the life God has called you. Maybe your attitude needs an adjustment.

You can be a witness. It doesn't have to be a dramatic change; start by handing out one tract a week. Make changes in your life so that you don't look like the world. Pray that you can be the kind of church member that measures up to the criteria scripture has laid out for us to be.

Be the kind of member who sees the church as a big deal.

CHAPTER SIX

"What's the Big Deal about the PURPOSE of the Church?"

Why did Jesus establish the church? What function was it created to fulfill? We see its purpose in Matthew 28:19-20, in what we refer to as the Great Commission—make disciples of the Lord Jesus Christ. This mission includes a personal conversion, public confession, and progressive confirmation.

It's a *great* commission because of its magnitude, message, meaning, motive, and miracles. We find it in Matthew 28, Luke 24, Mark 16, and John 20. It's recorded a fifth time in Acts1:8, which says, *"But ye shall receive power, after that the Holy Ghost is come upon you: and ye shall be witnesses unto me both in Jerusalem, and in all*

Judaea, and in Samaria, and unto the uttermost part of the earth."

What's the big deal about church? Simply put, its *purpose.* You may have preconceived ideas about the church, some negative ones that hinder you from surrendering to what God calls you to do. As we unpack what Scripture has to say, my prayer for you is that you would approach this lesson with an open heart, ready to receive this message.

It has been said that every local church is just one generation away from extinction.

Think of how many churches were regarded as great churches throughout history, yet today, they're closed. Once the missionary sending agency country in the world, England has countless churches who've shut their doors, and now they're converted into museums, shops, or even residences.

In Revelation chapters two and three, we hear a warning from the Lord to seven local churches in Asia minor—what is today western Turkey. God warns the church that if we do not repent from our error, if we do not return to our first love, Jesus Christ will remove the candlestick, and the church will cease to function Biblically. The church cannot live without the presence of the Lord Jesus Christ because the body cannot survive without the head. When a church is decapitated, it may function for a while; it may even have social activities and good times, but life is gone, and soon it will be nothing more than a corpse.

At my home church, we strive to keep the main thing, the main thing. More than 50 years ago, God called my father to the south side of Chicago to start a church so that they could make disciples of the Lord Jesus Christ. Unfortunately, within this generation of evangelicals, we hear so much on Christian radio and TV that distracts from evangelism by dumbing down the message of the gospel into little more than an emotional musical experience. There is no substitute for true worship and for glorifying God. There is no substitute for experiencing the presence of the Holy Spirit, but none of these things is a substitute for the church.

The *Ford Motor Company* used to advertise that quality was priority number one. While that may have been their priority, the purpose of the Ford Motor Company was to make automobiles. So it is with the church—glorifying God is priority number one. But, we exist to make disciples of the Lord Jesus Christ. And when the church fails to fulfill its purpose, it will soon die.

In the 18th century, the French infidel Voltaire proudly declared Christianity would be extinct within 100 years of his death. Yet, only 50 years after he died, a publishing company used his home to print Bibles. I like those kinds of stories, where the devil is so bold to say he's going to whip God, yet God flips the script and puts the evil one to shame.

Sadly, if you were to drive just a few miles south of my church, you'd come to a little village where my family lived for sixteen years. I could show you a beautiful library with incredible woodwork. It's warm and cozy, but sadly, it used to be a church. It didn't outgrow its facilities. In fact, just the opposite, it shrunk and withered up to nothing and died.

All across Europe, churches that at one time flourished with the gospel of Christ have become museums. That's what happens when churches don't keep the main thing, the main thing. We need a revival here and around the world. Look around your neighborhood, look around this church. The world needs Jesus Christ. But you know what you and I will do? We will run from this place back to the secret confines and the safety of our own home.

At my home church, several children started riding the church bus. Unfortunately, they don't behave as well as some of our members feel they should, disturbing those around them. Finally, someone dared to correct them. They've even been sent home from the services, yet, they continue to come. God is working in them. Some may be quick to condemn these children, while in truth, they're no better and no worse than children raised within the church. The only hope those kids have is Jesus, and the church is the key to that hope. It may be challenging, but we are committed to discipling children like these to become like Jesus Christ.

Consider the sanctioning of the mission. Sanction means the action of recognized authority, confirming or ratifying a decree, a command, or privilege. It's authoritative permission or approval that makes a course of action valid. Think of it as a law or statute. Missionary and explorer David Livingston once said, "If a commission by an earthly king is considered an honor, how can a commission by a Heavenly King be considered a sacrifice?"

As followers of Jesus Christ, we have been given a mission. We have authority given to us by the King of Kings to carry out His orders. It doesn't matter what the world says, what church growth books say, what people believe, or whether they want the gospel or not. The King of Kings has authorized us to spread the message that Jesus loves you and can save your soul.

Consider the soldiers of the mission. The words "ye shall" in Matthew 28:19-20 are addressed to us as a church. We have a purpose to fulfill, and that is to win souls. We must pull our monies, talents, programs, and activities together to tell others about Christ.

There's a family in my home church that hosts a harvest party for their friends and neighbors. First, they'll go through a great deal of work, cleaning up their barn. Then, everything will be set up for games, delicious food, and devotions. The purpose of the party is to bring unsaved and unchurched people into the family of God. It's an opportunity for them to be around believers and see that we're human, but we have something in us that makes us different. It's a "harvest" party, and we're hoping that we'll harvest the unsaved for the kingdom of God.

We, as a church, are called to be soldiers going out and reaching the lost. Charles Spurgeon said, "The fact is, brethren, we must have conversion work here. We cannot go on as some churches do without converts. We cannot, we will not, we must not, we dare not. Souls must be converted here, and if there be not many born to Christ, may the Lord grant to me that I may sleep in the tomb and be heard no more. Better indeed for us to die than to live, if souls be not saved."

When I was a child, I often heard references to the troops in Vietnam. I thought a troop was a group of about 20 men, but a troop is simply one soldier. Scripture gives a command to each member of God's army. The word "ye" in Matthew 28:18-19 is plural. God says every one of you shall be witnesses unto me. Not just the outspoken, not the intellectuals, not the charismatic, or those with charm and personality. Every one of you that names the name of Christ shall be a witness unto Him.

It is the responsibility of every follower of Christ to share the gospel of Jesus Christ. That is our mission. That is why we are here. Do you ever wonder what would happen to your church if every member made it a priority to bring someone to Christ this year? Do you know why some of you have never led a soul to Christ? Because you've never intended to. Let's be honest. Some of you have no intention of going out and telling someone about

Christ. "Well, preacher, I will if God presents to me an opportunity." Really?

What do you mean, "If God gives you an opportunity?" You have a mouth to speak, air in your lungs, the gospel of Jesus Christ, and the indwelling of the Holy Spirit. You are an opportunity waiting for a place to happen. But, unfortunately, some of you have never led a soul to Christ because you've never intended to, and that's why our world is getting darker and darker.

I am shocked at how many in our churches today think that if we just elect a conservative president, it will change America. This country is not going to change until people are changed from the inside out. The only way that will happen is if they get saved, and that can only happen if someone tells them about Jesus Christ. We are soldiers of the cross. You may not win them, but you can at least bring them to church, where they'll hear the gospel. You can pray for them and work together as a team. Somebody needs to rise up and say, "Listen, I've gone long enough without winning someone to Christ I'm going out, and I'm going to win someone to Jesus." The overly pious may say, "Well, it's not the work of man to save souls." True, it is the work of the Holy Spirit, but allow Him to use you. Somebody told you about Jesus, and we owe it to the lost to tell them.

Consider the source of the mission. "But ye shall receive power after the holy ghost has come upon you." Without the Spirit of God, we can do nothing. We are ships without wind, chariots without steeds, branches without sap, or dying coals without fire. We are useless as an offering without the sacrificial flame. We are unaccepted. Listen, the source is the Holy Spirit. Corrie ten Boom said, "Trying to do the Lord's word in your own strength is the most confusing, exhausting and tedious of all work. But when you are filled with the Holy Spirit, then the ministry of Jesus Christ flows right out of you."

Jesus promised us the Holy Spirit. He illuminates, He sheds light on Scripture, and He is the one who saves. The Holy Spirit convicts—not the preacher, not a dramatic production or a song— it's the Holy Spirit. It's the work of the Holy Spirit that speaks and moves the hearts of men and women. Zechariah 4:6 says, *"Not by might nor by power, but by my spirit says the Lord of hosts."* If we, as believers would just listen to the Holy Spirit and obey His prompting in our lives, we would be bold. We would be faithful in telling others about Jesus Christ.

Consider the scope of the mission. I love to read the story of Dwight L. Moody. While he was in London during one of his famous evangelistic tours, several British clergy members visited him. They wanted to know how this poorly educated American was so effective at winning throngs of people to Jesus Christ. So, Moody took those preachers with him to a window overlooking the city of London and said, "Describe for me what you see." One by one, the men described the people in the park down below. Moody looked out the window with tears rolling down his cheeks. One of the preachers asked, "What do you see?" Moody replied, "I see countless thousands of souls that will one day spend eternity in hell if they do not find the savior." Moody saw people differently from the average person on the street because he saw them as eternal souls. He was daily motivated to reach them with the gospel of Jesus Christ.

Every soul has a body. And until you look at every person you meet as a soul that will spend eternity somewhere, it's unlikely you'll win anybody. Whether wealthy or poor, a scholar or an athlete, everyone we encounter will spend eternity somewhere. Therefore, we all need Jesus Christ, and until we can see men and women as eternal souls, we aren't likely to do anything about it.

We have to be intentional about winning souls. When farmers harvest their crops, they plan every step. They work the fields, watch for the crops to ripen, then go out into the field for harvest. So likewise, if we plan, we will win souls and be more productive in bringing people to Christ. Many Christians have lost sight of the fact that God still desires people to come to a saving knowledge of Jesus Christ. Some may say it's too hard to win souls in this postmodern culture. Can I say it kindly? It's always been hard. God isn't looking for results. He's looking for obedience. If we do our part, He will do his part. The more seed that we sow, the greater the harvest we will reap. We ought to attempt something so great for God that unless He intervenes, we're bound to fail. Baptist missionary William Carey once said, "Expect great things for God; attempt great things from God."

Yes, expect great things from God. In Paul Powell's book, *The Complete Disciple*, he describes the condition of the average church today:

> *"Many churches today remind me of a laboring crew trying to gather in a harvest while they sit in the tool shed. They go to the tool shed every Sunday and they*

study bigger and better methods of agriculture, sharpen their hoes, grease their tractors, and then get up and go home. Then they come back that night, study bigger and better methods of agriculture, sharpen their hoes, grease their tractors, and go home again. They comeback Wednesday night, and again study bigger and better methods of agriculture, sharpen their hoes, grease their tractors, and get up and go home. They do this week in and week out, year in and year out, and nobody ever goes out into the fields to gather in the harvest."

I've been on the other side of this sermon, and I remember saying to myself, "But I have tried." Because I've tried, there have been times I've excused myself from continuing to pursue someone I've shared the gospel with over and over. Don't give up. Don't stop sharing the gospel. You don't have to try to win the same person every time, nor do you have to approach them the same way every time.

Some of you may have wayward children, and you can't figure out how to reach them. I would suggest that if anyone can reach your children, it's you. They need to see Jesus Christ in you, and that means humbling yourself. You're not going to win your adult children by barking at them, but you can by loving them and telling them how Christ is working in your life today. Your children might have a chance if they could see their parents humbled, submitting to godly authority. That would be a template for them to pattern their life after. You'll see them say, "If my dad, or if my mom can humble themselves and submit to biblical authority, then I should too." Some of us have crazy neighbors or ungodly family members.

They need Jesus.

Why don't you invite them to your home for dinner? Why don't you take them out for lunch sometime and build a relationship with them? You may say, "Oh, but I'm busy." I know that's my excuse, too, sometimes. But if I want to win them to Christ, I will be intentional in my efforts.

If your kids are in public school, your kids are being indoctrinated by the world for six hours a day. Even if they have Christian teachers, the world is influencing them. If there's ever a family that needs to be proactive, it's the families that have their children in public schools. It can be done and should be done. Plan an activity where they bring their friends to your house. Have fun, but also demonstrate a testimony of what's different in your home. You may say, "Well, the kids won't like it." This isn't about whether they like it or not. If they're unsaved, of course, they're not going to like it. That's part of our sinful nature. But the only way they're ever going to hear the gospel is for someone to love them and show them that Jesus Christ cares for them. You might win one. You might win two.

Recently, my family got word that one of our daughter's childhood friends had come to faith as an adult. The harvest took a while, but it came back because the seed was sown years ago.

Ask yourself, "How can I present the gospel to someone? How can I show them that God loves them?" Simple: think, pray, plan, and ask, "Will you join me at church on Sunday?" We need to pray for revival in soul-winning in our local churches. We're to keep the main thing, the main thing. We must see souls saved regularly so that the church will be filled with new converts, or as Spurgeon asked: "Why have church?"

The church must become a very big deal to us.

CHAPTER SEVEN

"What's the Big Deal about the PEOPLE of the Church?"

When the apostle John was banished to the deserted island of Patmos because of his faithful stand for Jesus Christ, he had a powerful experience of God's power and grace.

John had been one of Jesus' twelve original disciples. He was also one of the three who were part of His inner circle. John walked with Jesus for three and a half years, hearing Him teach, and seeing Him perform miracles. During his own ministry, John himself performed miracles. He sat beside Jesus Christ at the last supper and is commonly believed to be the disciple whom Jesus loved, referred to in John 13:23, John 19:26, and John 21:7.

John saw Jesus Christ transfigured into His heavenly glory on a mountain top. So, being imprisoned on a desolate island didn't cheat him. John had already experienced so many profound things—far more than any of us will ever experience on earth. Even in his loneliest hour on Patmos, John had a treasure chest of memories he could draw from as he was waiting to die.

Why would a Roman government imprison a frail man, likely in his 80s? Why would they eventually dip him in boiling oil? It was because he was a threat to the leadership of the realm.

But God was still in control of John's story, even in his most desperate hour. He was yet to experience even more of God's grace. In fact, God revealed the next 2000 years of history to John and told him to write what he saw. John was privileged to see the revelation of Jesus Christ. God further commissioned John to write seven letters to seven local churches in Asia minor—Ephesus, Smyrna, Pergamum Thyatira, Sardis, Philadelphia, and Laodicea.

Many students of the Bible believe those local churches also represent seven distinct periods of church history, with Laodicea marking the generation before the rapture, as described in Revelation chapter four. It may or may not be true that these churches represent seven periods in church history. But it seems clear to me that most churches in America today resemble the church in Laodicea. They're lukewarm—not hot, not cold—and they make Jesus sick.

The word Laodicea literally means "people rule" or "the rights of the people." Today there is a great distaste for authority, even in the church of the living God. It may result from corruption in the home, church, or government, coupled with the depraved nature of man, one that resists authority. On the other hand, it could spring from an over-educated society filled with people who think they are equal with God and His ordained authority. I'm not sure how America has sunk so low, but the final words of the Old Testament Book of Judges could be the epitaph for our age, even in churches: *"Every man did that which was right in his own eyes."*

It says in Hebrews 13:17, *"Obey them that have the rule over you, and submit yourselves: for they watch for your souls, as they that must give account, that they may do it with joy, and not with grief: for that is unprofitable for you."* When we get saved, baptized, and added to a local church, becoming good church members to glorify the Lord is the next step.

I once read a story about a pastor who learned the cold, hard truth about one of his members who appeared to be a great saint on Sunday mornings. He saw her in traffic, and she was stressed-out and tailgating someone. Suddenly the light turned yellow and driver in front did the right thing, stopping at the crosswalk, even though he could have beaten the red light by accelerating through the intersection. The tailgating woman was furious. She honked her horn and screamed with frustration because she missed her chance to get through the intersection.

The woman heard a tap on her window, and when she looked up, she saw the stern looking face of a police officer. The officer ordered her to get out of her car, He then arrested her and took her to the police station, where she was searched, fingerprinted, photographed, and placed in a holding cell. After a couple of hours, a policeman opened the door, and she was escorted back to the booking desk where the arresting officer was waiting with her personal effects. He greeted her and said, "I'm very sorry for the mistake. You see, I pulled up behind your car while you were blowing your horn, flipping off the guy in front of you and cussing a blue streak at him. I noticed your 'What would Jesus do?' bumper sticker, the choose life license plate holder, the 'Follow me to Sunday

School' bumper sticker, and the chrome-plated Christian fish emblem on the trunk. So naturally, I assumed that you had stolen the car."

Being a Christian and a member of a local church carries with it some responsibility. The Bible details how members should behave. It outlines how we can glorify God. And it tells us the things we should avoid.

When people join my church, they generally ask, "Pastor, is there anything I can do?" My answer usually is, "Yes, there are at least seven basic things that pastors want every church member to learn as they grow in grace."

First, every pastor wants their church members to *read the Bible*. Choose a Bible-believing, Bible-preaching, Bible-practicing, Bible-studying church because the Bible is food for the soul of every believer. The Bible is the final authority for the church, home, and every nation that desires the blessings of God. Church members should read their Bible every single day. Generally, when you make a statement like that, people will say, "Well, how much should I read? Do I read the whole Bible in one night?" Well, if you can, yes. But if you need a week, take a week—take a year, but read the whole Bible from cover to cover and read it every single day.

You may decide to read ten chapters—you may choose to read thirty chapters. Some of you may say, "Wait a minute. I can't even read!" Well, you can get the audio version and listen to it. Turn off the television. Don't try to iron. Don't try to play basketball. Sit and listen to the Word of God being read to you if you can't read it yourself. You may say, "Well, thirty chapters a day is an awful lot to read." Then, start with one single verse—just read something every day from God's Word.

It says in 2 Timothy 2:15, *"Study to show yourself approved under God, a workman that needeth not to be ashamed, rightly dividing the word of truth."* Psalm 119:11 says, *"Thy word, have I hid in mine heart that I might not sin against thee."* As believers in Christ, we should hide God's word in our hearts because we desire not to sin against God. In John 5:9, Jesus challenges us to search the scriptures. Psalm 1:2 says, *"His delight is in the law of the Lord. And in his law, does he meditate day and night."*

Second, *pray daily*. Believers must develop a prayer life and learn to pray for other church members, even if you may not know them personally. We are members of the same body, so we ought to pray for one another. I pray for people I know, even though I don't see every need in their life. I can't possibly know every need, but I can still pray fervently for them.

The Spirit of God takes my prayers and interprets them before the throne of God. God answers them according to His will. Throughout Scripture, we are taught the importance of prayer. The Apostle Paul tells us to "*pray without ceasing*" in 1 Thessalonians 5:17. Jesus said in Luke 18:1 that *"men ought always to pray and not to faint."* Philippians 4:6 says, *"Be careful for nothing; but in everything by prayer and supplication with thanksgiving let your requests be made known unto God."* 1 Timothy 2:1 challenges us, *"I exhort therefore, that, first of all, supplications, prayers, intercessions, and giving of thanks, be made for all men."* In Matthew 26:41, Jesus says, *"Watch and pray that you enter not into temptation."* 1 Samuel 12:23 warns, *"Moreover, as for me, God forbid that I should sin against the Lord in ceasing to pray for you."*

To develop your prayer life, I suggest starting a prayer journal. It could be a notebook, a document on your computer, a note in your phone— just create a list and write down the names of people for whom you're praying. Jot down notes of the needs that they have. Put a date by them, and then when God answers that prayer, record the date so for years to come you can praise Him for it. Do this every day.

Third, every church member should attend church services faithfully. In Hebrews 10:25, there is a challenge with the words, *"Not forsaking the assembling of ourselves together, as the manner of some is; but exhorting one another: and so much the more, as ye see the day approaching."*

If there's ever been a day we need to be in church, if there's ever been a day the world needs to see us in church, it's now—during these dark hours as the return of Jesus Christ draws near. It says in 1 Corinthians 12:12, *"For as the body is one, and hath many members, and all the members of that one body, being many, are one body: so also is Christ."* Every member is important. Every member needs to be present. When people get out of sorts and excuse themselves for their absenteeism, they often get a chip on the shoulder and talk as if they know more than the preacher. They will say, "Well, I don't have to go to church to worship God." That's an attitude problem. Your body is the temple of the Holy Spirit. The early church had to go to the temple to worship God, but our body is the temple, thanks to Jesus' sacrifice at Calvary. At the moment of salvation, the Holy Spirit indwells us as believers.

We should be worshipers of God, 24 hours a day, seven days a week. When believers who have worshiped the Lord all week long come together on Sunday morning, the atmosphere can be electric. When a church service is flat, mark it down, it's because the members have not been worshiping the Lord throughout the week. They're relying on the church to bail them out and be a spiritual cheerleader to get them fired up for another week.

The church ought to be a place of revival, but the truth of the matter is the preacher isn't responsible for your walk with the Lord. You are. When an unsaved man walks into a church, he ought to sense the spirit of God Almighty indwelling and filling the place before a word is uttered. For those who have backslidden away from God and feel disheartened and disillusioned, the church should be an oasis to the thirsty soul who knows God and knows better. We must be faithful. It's not a legalistic position—it's Bible doctrine.

Faithfulness to a Bible-believing church is important, and it's not all about you, and it's not all about me. It is about God and His honor and glory. We must not send confusing signals to a lost world.

The fourth thing a pastor wants his people to do is *give tithes and offerings*. God says in Malachi 3:10, *"Bring ye all the tithes into the storehouse, that there may be meat in mine house, and prove me now herewith, saith the Lord of hosts, if I will not open you the windows of heaven, and pour you out a blessing, that there shall not be room enough to receive it."*

My dad used to talk about the millions, even billions, of dollars that have been sent to religious organizations. Had that money been sent to the local church, there would be no need in any local church ministry. So, God tells us to test Him, saying, "I know you love money, and I know it's hard for you to let go, but I want you to try me on this one. Give me your tithe, and see if I will not open you the windows of heaven and pour you out a blessing so great there will not be room enough to receive it."

I never had access to the giving records of church members. I do not know how much the people give for several reasons. I think I'm spiritual a lot of the time, but not *all* the time, and if I find out that someone is not tithing, I might have a bad attitude towards them. Why? Because if they'll steal and cheat on God, they will steal and cheat on me or someone else in the church. It's a proven fact. The only person mentioned in the Bible who criticized the Lord for spending money was Judas Iscariot. He was a thief and a church officer—in fact, he was the treasurer.

I don't look at the church giving records because I don't need to know who gives the big bucks, though I can guess they're often not the people driving the nicest cars. Do you know how I can guess? Because Jesus said where your treasure is, that's where your heart will be. And people who love God's work don't mind giving money, time, and energy to His work.

If you love steak, you don't mind shelling out a little extra for a good one. Perhaps you love a specific car model, and even though it costs a little more, you don't mind because you love that car. So likewise, people who love God do not mind giving to Him. On the contrary, they welcome the thought of giving to God and His work.

Jesus had twelve disciples, but there were three particular men within His inner circle. Jesus didn't have favorites—God loves us all equally—but three of His disciples had a closer relationship with Him than the others. And within that three, there was one Jesus referred to as the beloved disciple, the one who loved Him the most.

The Bible says in 2 Corinthians 9:6, *"But this I say, He which soweth sparingly shall reap also sparingly; and he which soweth bountifully shall reap also bountifully. Every man according as he purposeth in his heart, so let him give; not grudgingly, or of necessity: for God loveth a cheerful giver."* It's incredible how He opens the windows of heaven. You may wonder how it happens, but God loves a cheerful giver and He loves to bless His children.

In Luke 6:38, Jesus said, *"Give, and it shall be given unto you; good measure, pressed down, and shaken together, and running over, shall men give into your bosom. For with the same measure that ye mete withal it shall be measured to you again."*

Again, tithing simply means giving 10% of your total gross income. Tithing is not only commanded— it is *rewarded.* I would remind each follower of Christ that if you haven't learned to tithe, you're not only robbing God, but you are robbing yourself of so many blessings.

Fifth, as church members, we should help with the *maintenance of the church.* Sadly, some church members treat the house of God with far less respect than they do their own homes. They sit in services chewing gum, and when they're through, they stick it under their pew or in the seat pocket meant for a hymnal. It's thrown on the asphalt in the parking lot, sticking to the bottom of shoes, and tracked in on the carpet. Others have been known to sit in their pew clipping their nails, as if that task has to be done at that moment. The cleaners come through and have to pick up their clippings off the floor and pews.

In Acts 6:2-3, the apostle Paul said, *"Then the twelve called the multitude of the disciples unto them, and said, It is not reason that we should leave the word of God, and serve tables. Wherefore, brethren, look ye out among you seven men of honest report, full of the Holy Ghost and wisdom, whom we may appoint over this business."* I know some people think the preacher only works on Sunday but preparing a sermon to preach God's word involves more than just study. There's a time of prayer to prepare the preacher as well as the message.

My church is blessed to be maintained exclusively by volunteers. Now that may not always be the case. I understand that some may grow weary and need to step down, and I wouldn't want anyone to feel guilty when they can't do it anymore. But we could all help a little bit, even on Sundays. If you see that the countertop is wet or the sink is messy, just grab a paper towel and wipe them down so that the next person that comes will have a nice clean area to wash their hands. If you see a piece of paper on the floor, pick it up and throw it away. It's good to keep our facilities as nice as we possibly can for the glory of the Lord.

Sixth, church members should be soul winners. Acts 1:8 says, *"But ye shall receive power, after that the Holy Ghost is come upon you: and ye shall be witnesses unto me both in Jerusalem, and in all Judaea, and in Samaria, and unto the uttermost part of the earth."*

Yes, we must be engaged in missions and spread the gospel to Judea and Samaria, but we also have a responsibility here at home. God forbid that we'd send missionaries across the ocean but not take it across the street. There are people around us who need Jesus Christ. Proverbs 11:30 says, *"The fruit of the righteous is a tree of life. And he that wins souls is wise."* Since the purpose of our church is to make disciples of the Lord Jesus Christ, we should all be involved in witnessing.

I know some people may be introverted, and some feel like they've never been trained to be a soul winner for Jesus Christ, but all of us can witness. There are four different ways that you can witness. First, you can give somebody a gospel tract. You don't have to say a word;

just say, "Would you please read this?" For example, you can give them to your server at a restaurant—just leave it on the table, or better yet, you can engage with your server. Make sure you give them a good tip. Slip it inside the tract, and say, "Would you please read this?" That'll make a more significant impact than just leaving it on the table.

Second, invite someone to church. You may say, how's that a form of witnessing? Those of you who have unsaved friends and family know what I'm talking about. An invitation to church seems simple, but it can be uncomfortable because they may not respond the way we'd like. Invite someone to church with you—that in itself is a witness. When they come to the house of God, they're going to be around God's people and sense the Spirit of God in the preaching of the Word.

Thirdly, pray with somebody about their soul. Every year for our Thanksgiving dinner, my wife Laurie puts Thanksgiving verses of Scripture at each place setting. We read the Scripture and pray for our food, but if we have any unsaved guests, we pray for their eternal destiny like this: "Oh dear God, thank you for saving our souls. If there's someone here today that doesn't know Christ as savior, we hope and pray that they'll be saved before they die."

Now, that seems so simple for you and me, but an unsaved person is likely thinking, "What's he talking about?" The spirit of God will then be able to work with them. If you visit a friend in the hospital, you can pray for them, but you can also pray for their roommate. Just ask, "What is your name? I want to say a prayer for you, is that all right?" I have yet to be refused for that. I pray for their health, and I pray they get to go home soon. But even more importantly, I pray that this person comes to know Jesus Christ as their personal savior.

Fourth, give people the gospel. Use the Romans Road, use the Book of John, but even if you don't know any particular plan on how to present the gospel, you can tell them how you got saved.

I was just a young boy, only eight years old, when I heard a preacher preaching revival at the Akron Baptist Temple. I didn't understand it all, but I knew one thing: I knew I was dying and going to hell at eight years old. What can an eight-year-old do that's bad enough to send them to hell? I was born with man's depraved nature, and I intentionally and deliberately of my own volition violated and transgressed against the Word of God. As soon as I crossed that line, I had a guilty conscience. And when I heard the Spirit of God speaking to me directly through that preacher, I knew I was unfit for heaven. Even as an eight-year-old boy, I understood that. I heard that Jesus Christ died for my sins. He was buried, then rose again from the grave. I didn't understand all the theology behind it, but I believed that He died for me, and I believe He wanted to save me. So, I said, "Dear Jesus, save me." And He did—He saved me at eight years old. I've never been the same since.

God wants every church member to witness. We can't set goals for how many people we win to Christ because that's the work of the Holy Spirit, but we should strive to witness to as many for Christ as we can. We're not salesmen. We're not trying to get people to bow their heads so we can say, "I led another one to Christ." No, but we are to be witnesses, and if we are willing, God will use us to win people to Jesus Christ.

Finally, every member ought to be *involved in a church ministry*. Ephesians 4:11-12 says, *"And he gave some, apostles; and some, prophets; and some, evangelists; and some, pastors and teachers; For the perfecting of the saints, for the work of the ministry, for the edifying of the body of Christ."* The happiest people in any church are those who are involved in ministry. Over the years, I've had people join our church who believe it's God's will. They're excited. They enjoy it, and they comment on the spirit of the church. They love the music. They love the missionary program. They even like the pastor.

Then after a while, because they don't get involved in a ministry, they feel disjointed and disconnected. They begin to feel like they really don't have any close friends in the church. Before long, they get upset about something that's gone wrong in their life. And because they're not connected to anyone, there's no one to rally behind them and support them through a difficult time. They say, "Where is the church?" In truth, they're mad at God, but it's easier to get angry at the church.

But often, the reason is that they're not involved in ministry. Some of the best friendships in the church are made when men and women are deep in the trenches, vacuuming, soul winning, or teaching Sunday School. They're bringing kids in on the church bus, mowing grass, singing in the choir.

The best friendships that we make in this life are when we are rubbing shoulders with others that are doing the work of God. You may say, "But preacher, I'm not gifted like you. I'm not like so-and-so. I could never do such a thing." But, if God has saved you, He has called you, and if He has called you, He will equip you.

We should not remain immature Christians all our life. Babies can't live on milk or formula forever, and likewise, as believers in Christ, we should have the desire to get into the meat of the word. Get involved in the ministry. There may be barriers that stand in your way—family problems, financial struggles, stress at work—but realize the problems of this world will always try to pull your eyes off the high calling of Jesus Christ. If you do right by God, you might be surprised at what He will do in your home.

Examine your heart. Do you read your Bible every day? Have you read your Bible from cover to cover? If you've been saved for more than five years, the answer should be yes. If you haven't, there's little wonder you're starving spiritually. Do you have a real prayer life where you could stand and testify what God has done for you? Do you attend church faithfully? Do you tithe, do you help maintain the church? Do you witness, are you involved in ministry?

I'm not here to judge you. I'm required of the Lord to lead the people of God under me in my ministry, and

I believe the same truths apply to all believers. They are biblically sound and healthy for every local church.

It's all part of how we can all make the church a big deal.

CHAPTER EIGHT

"What's the Big Deal about the PRAISE of the Church"

One year, I wanted to help my wife with the cooking for Thanksgiving dinner. I volunteered to stuff the turkey.

The turkey shot out of the oven, and rocketed into the air.
It knocked every plate off the table and partly demolished the chair.
It ricocheted into a corner and bust with a deafening boom,
Then splattered all over the kitchen, completely obscuring the room.
It stuck to the walls and the windows, it totally coated the floor,

There was turkey attached to the ceiling, where they'd never been turkey before.
It blanketed every appliance, it smeared every saucer and bowl,
There wasn't a way I could stop it, that turkey was out of control.
I scraped and I scrubbed with displeasure, and thought with sorrow as I mopped,
That I'd never again stuff a turkey with popcorn that had not been popped.

Sometimes the best help you can offer is praise to the work of someone who knows what they are doing. And since we are talking about the church, it's appropriate that we consider *praise in the church,* which reminds us why the church is a big deal.

In Luke 19:37-40 it says, *"And when he was come nigh, even now at the descent of the mount of Olives, the whole multitude of the disciples began to rejoice and praise God with a loud voice for all the mighty works that they had seen: saying, 'Blessed be the King that cometh in the name of the Lord: peace in heaven, and glory in the highest.' And some of the Pharisees from among the multitude said unto him, 'Master, rebuke thy disciples.' And he answered and said unto them, 'I tell you that, if these should hold their peace, the stones would immediately cry out.'"*

These verses take place on what we call Palm Sunday, the week before Easter Sunday, or resurrection Sunday. It takes place when the Lord is entering into the city of Jerusalem just a few days before He is to be crucified. I want to single out just two words of this quote. "Praise God!"

The great prophet, Isaiah, in chapter 53 of his book, said that Jesus Christ was a man of sorrows. Kids today don't understand how they have it made in the shade compared to when we were there.

I had a Bible professor who used to say that he was not convinced that Jesus ever laughed. And the reason for that was Isaiah 53. Jesus was a man of sorrows. Jesus could see the hearts of men and women. He knew what was really going on inside and He was broken hearted over the sad, sorrowful, sinful condition of each man and woman. We only see the exterior.

Though I agree with that professor, that Jesus is the man of sorrows, I also know that no man has been anointed with a nobler, purer, and deeper joy than the Lord Jesus Christ.

It says in Acts 20:35, *"It is more blessed to give than to receive."* Each step to Calvary brought with it a joy and excitement of what would soon be given to this world. Jacob labored seven years for the right to marry Rachel. In Genesis 29:20 it says, *"And they seemed unto him but a few days, for the love he had to her."*

So it is with Jesus, who gave His life for us with joy, because He loves us.

I want to challenge you to praise God. Praise God from whom ALL blessings flow. I have two thoughts about praising God that I want to share with you. First, *there will always be Pharisees who want to squash a praise gathering.*

In Luke 19:39 it says, *"And some of the Pharisees from among the multitude said unto him, 'Master, rebuke thy disciples.'"* When we deliberately decide to praise God, as these passionate disciples did, we will always encounter Pharisees.

Why do I say that? Why would religious people who know the Bible object to praising God? Does that make sense?

Let me tell you why this is true. First, because there is no praise for them. It bothers Pharisees to think that someone other than them, their family, or their approved friends, could get credit and recognition and be exalted above them. Pastors are often fearful about praising any particular member of the church because of the Pharisees in the crowd that will say, "Why does he praise him and not me?" So, we just do our best to thank people on a personal level, and then praise God from the pulpit. We don't want to burden those poor pharisees in the multitude.

Second, Pharisees are jealous of happy people. No one is happy all the time. When I go through periods of unhappiness, the last thing I want to hear is someone shouting, "Praise God." The last thing I want is to feel convicted about being unhappy, and be around someone who just loves Jesus and all that superficial reality and emotionalism. I want them to be a realist. I want them to deal with the cold, hard fact that this world is miserable. And I'm part of this miserable world. And I'm contributing to the miserableness of this world.

We all know people like this. Pharisees are not happy people. They are lonely and unhappy. Now, they may *say* they are happy, but deep down they cannot stand to see others who are truly happy.

Instead, if we can't rejoice and be happy, then we should be glad there are others who can. The prodigal son's older brother became mad because his father had a welcome home party for his sinful, younger brother. He cried to his dad, "You never gave me a party like this!"

Third, Pharisees are jealous of Jesus. The Pharisees could not accept that people were happy in the temple and happy with Jesus. They had the audacity to go to Jesus and ask Him to knock it off. Sadly, there are people like this in our churches today. I've known of people in church who prayed that God would stop any joy and happiness in the church.

In the 1980s, my dad's health was weakening and he had had all he could take. One of our deacons complained about clapping in the service. Now this seems funny today, but it wasn't then. He thought it was disrespectful. Even though the Bible tells us, *Clap your hands unto the Lord.* I've always wondered how people can get upset when something is in the Bible? Don't like drums? They are in the Bible. Don't like people shouting amen? It's in the Bible. Don't like when people shout praise the Lord? It's in the Bible.

Yet the Pharisees had the boldness to pray and ask Jesus to stop the praising. This is because they did not want Christ crowned as King. All the Pharisees loved preaching about holy living because they thought they were pretty good at it. They loved preaching about separation—that's what the word "pharisee" actually means. They thought they were pretty good at that. They loved preaching on the authority of the Bible.

Today, we have people who love to hear sermons from the King James Version of the Bible. So do I, but Pharisees do not like to hear a message on the Lordship of Jesus Christ, where He gets preeminence.

It's not about me. It's not about you. It is all about Him. We lift up Jesus Christ as Lord. We don't lift up a man. We don't lift up a family. We don't even lift up the United States of America. Yes. We're thankful to be an American. But the truth of the matter is God loves people all over the world.

I remember my dad came to the pulpit and he said, "Folks, I had someone come to me and say that they do not like the clapping in our singing. So, I'm going to tell you right now, knock it off. And don't come running up to me after the service, asking who it is that is making the fuss. We're going to surrender our rights. And for expediency, we will stop clapping in church."

That was a day when the joy and shout was gone from church. The devil's Pharisees robbed the church of her joy and strength. Why? Because the joy of the Lord is our strength. When we're happy in the Lord, we're ready to serve Him with all our strength.

Second, *praising God is Scriptural.* Praise is a blessing to God and to His people. Praise is a response from a thankful heart. Luke 19:40 says, *"If these should hold their peace, their stones would immediately cry."* Jesus was telling them that when a man or a woman is full of thanks for what God has done, they cannot help but praise God. We that belong to God SHOULD be thankful.

We are thankful because it honors Him.

We are thankful because it obeys His word.

We are thankful because it helps us to avoid dangerous consequences.

We are thankful because it helps us not to be dependent on man for our happiness.

Instead, we are focused on the One who is the source of all happiness.

In Luke 19:37, we see that it was a speedy praise. "*And when he was come nigh.*" As the Lord approached Jerusalem, the crowds saw Him and immediately praised Him. They couldn't wait for Him to come. They were waiting for His coming. We also wait for Him today. We wait for His return, because He is coming again. We don't have to wait until He returns to experience His presence. The Bible says that He doesn't sleep. He is there when we wake up in the morning and He is there all night when we are sleeping.

We should praise Him when the day begins. We should praise Him when the church service begins. We should praise Him when the singing begins. We should praise Him when the sermon begins.

Many years ago, we used to sing out of a book called *Great Hymns of the Faith*. That was the hymnal we used. I directed music out of that book for a long time. It got to the point where I had a lot of the pages memorized. I barely needed the book. Number 498 was "When We All Get to Heaven." I loved that one because it was about rejoicing. When we come into church, we should be anticipating the presence of the Lord. And when we hear the song begin, we are joyful to praise Him in music.

When the preacher tells us to open our Bibles, there ought to be some praise. We go to a church that teaches and preaches the Word of God. We are not concerned about what a denomination has to say. We don't care what the TV preachers or the newspapers say. We want to hear what the Word of God says. And we praise Him when the preacher starts a sermon with the Word of God.

It was a speedy praise.

In Luke 19:37, we also see that *it was unanimous praise. "The whole multitude of the disciples."* It wasn't just one person, but a whole group. Now, some people are scared or shy or uncomfortable with praise, especially in public. They claim that they aren't very expressive.

I have an idea. Let's put their hand in a car door and just slam it Then we will see how expressive they can be. You may object, saying, that's just a response. Well, so is Praise. When a man is filled and blessed of the Lord, praise is our response.

The whole group praised Him! This group of people did not live perfect lives. They also had problems, trials and tribulations.

Our praise is not dependent on circumstances. It is not dependent on others. It is not dependent on the weather. It does not depend on finances. In fact, if you have nothing to praise God for, then help someone else to praise Him. Rejoice in other peoples' blessings. Praise Him for who He is, and not just for what He has done.

It was an exclusive praise. It was the whole multitude, but not the Pharisees. They were never happy. In the second verse of the hymn, *Marching to Zion*, it says, *"let those refuse to sing who never knew our God."*

It was a joyful praise. You don't have to be a good singer. All you need is a joyful heart. Some think that joyfulness is dangerous. That it is irreverent. That it can be a ruinous vice. Others say that it is shallow and temporal. But in Nehemiah 8:10, God says the joy of the Lord is our *strength*.

It was a loud praise. In Luke 19:37 it says, "Praise God with a loud voice." Many of us don't mind singing, but we don't want to sing out loud, in front of others. But that was not the case in verse 37. Their praise was the result of zeal, agreement, and alertness. There was expectation and anticipation in those disciples to see the Lord. And common to that expectation, they burst out into animated praise.

It was reasonable praise. Verse 37 also says, *"For all the mighty works that they had seen."* Have you ever noticed that when a guy hits a home run, the crowd goes wild? The crowd praises him. But in the church that kind of excitement and praise makes a lot of people uncomfortable.

Jesus is worthy of our praise!

He created the world. Jesus was born of a virgin. Jesus lived a sinless life. Jesus died for your sins. Jesus rose from the grave. Jesus saves, converts, and indwells sinners who call on His name. He is worthy of all praise!

It was personal praise. Though it was the whole multitude that praised Him, that multitude was made up of individuals. Individuals who loved, honored, worshipped and were expecting Jesus.

On November 18, 2006, I was sitting with more than 103,000 fans in Columbus, Ohio's famous *Horseshoe*—the football stadium famous for what had been advertised as the game of the century between the Ohio State Buckeyes and the University of Michigan Wolverines. I cannot exaggerate the loudness of the cheers from the fans in the stadium before the game even began. And when Coach Jim Trussel came out, followed by those young athletes running onto the field, those 103,000 fans roared in praise. The cheers were deafening.

You may be thinking that should be expected. It's the home of the Buckeyes.

So it should be in Church. A church without praise is a church without the presence of Jesus (Psalm 22:3). Just because we gather together, does not mean that Jesus will show up. But if we gather together in His name, He will be there. God is anywhere where two or three are gathered in His name. We can enjoy the presence of Christ in our praise.

When Jesus was near, they burst out in praise and rejoicing. Is Jesus near to your heart? We worship what we love. We praise what we worship. Let me put it this way: What we hear people praising and repeating this regularly reveals what the worship and what they love—what is nearest to their heart. The church that loves and worships God praises Him!

Praise is a vital way to answer the question: "What's the big deal about the church?"

ABOUT THE AUTHOR

Rev. Bruce M. Humbert was born in Canton, Ohio in 1953. He was *Born Again* in his home in 1961 after revival services at historic Akron Baptist Temple, where he was later baptized. In 1968 his family moved to Park Forest, IL, where his father started the Sauk Trail Baptist Temple.

Pastor Humbert trained for the ministry at Baptist Bible College in Springfield, Missouri. He graduated in 1974 with a degree in music. A few weeks after graduation, he married his high school sweetheart, Laurie Reinbold. God has blessed them with five daughters and eleven grandchildren.

Bruce served a few years as a youth and music director, first for a church in Texas, and then for his father at Sauk Trail Baptist Temple. When his father passed away in 1989, the church called Bruce to be their senior pastor—a post he held for 30 years. During his pastorate, more than $9 million was given to missions.

He has also preached at hundreds of special meetings around the country and in nearly 20 foreign countries. Though he has retired from the pastorate, his itinerant preaching continues on.

Pastor Humbert's favorite quote from scripture is from Galatians 2:20, "*...who loved me, and gave Himself for me.*"

His favorite subject to preach about is Missions, and he loves Laurie, his five baby girls and eleven grandchildren, and their home. He loves Baskin World Class Chocolate Robbins ice cream, extra sweet corn on the cob, Fogo de Chao, the Cleveland Indians (a.k.a. Guardians), and THE Ohio State Buckeyes.

Oh—and he has also rocked a cool handlebar mustache since 1978.

Made in the USA
Monee, IL
11 June 2023

35593803R00089